Advance praise for "What

Through her insightful connection and endless compassion, Sandy delivers an inspiring message of hope and love that readers everywhere will benefit from hearing. With heartfelt honesty, openness and a truth that is poignant beyond words, this compelling dialog offers answers that so many of us have searched for and a place of wisdom from which we can all begin to heal and truly live in peace.

> – Michele Lazcano, Emmy Award winning TV Producer & Co-Founder of LiveLifeFulfilled.com

*"What was God Thinking?!"* is the author's powerful ongoing conversations with God. There is no doubt that her relationship with God is real, deep and profound. She asks the questions and God answers-not always in the way you would expect! Sandy shares from her heart and the deepest part of her soul. I loved her down to earth voice and humor. This book is a must read. I couldn't put the book down, I wanted more of the wisdom and love that was coming right from God through Sandy.

> – Pat Hastings,MS,LCDP Author, Inspirational Speaker, Spiritual Coach, Radio Talk Show Host

*"What was God Thinking?!"* is a wonderfully wise, warm and insightful book. It will make life richer and happier for all those who read it. A remarkable work of trust in God from a remarkable woman. Sandy has given us all a precious and generous gift.

> – Linda L. Pestana Author of "Voices of the Heart"

For John + Lea,
May this be a
reminder of how truly
loved you are,
With love,
Sandy

# What was God

# Thinking?!

## I WANTED TO KNOW...
## SO I ASKED.

A HEART-WARMING DIALOG FOR THE JOURNEY BACK TO LOVE.

## SANDY ALEMIAN

**BALBOA**
PRESS

A DIVISION OF HAY HOUSE

Balboa Press books may be ordered through booksellers or by contacting:

Balboa Press
A Division of Hay House
1663 Liberty Drive
Bloomington, IN 47403
www.balboapress.com
1-(877) 407-4847

Because of the dynamic nature of the Internet, any Web addresses or links contained in this book may have changed since publication and may no longer be valid. The views expressed in this work are solely those of the author and do not necessarily reflect the views of the publisher, and the publisher hereby disclaims any responsibility for them.

The author of this book does not dispense medical advice or prescribe the use of any technique as a form of treatment for physical, emotional, or medical problems without the advice of a physician, either directly or indirectly. The intent of the author is only to offer information of a general nature to help you in your quest for emotional and spiritual well-being. In the event you use any of the information in this book for yourself, which is your constitutional right, the author and the publisher assume no responsibility for your actions.

Any people depicted in stock imagery provided by Thinkstock are models, and such images are being used for illustrative purposes only.
Certain stock imagery © Thinkstock.

ISBN: 978-1-4525-0144-4 (sc)
ISBN: 978-1-4525-2966-0 (dj)
ISBN: 978-1-4525-0145-1 (e)

Library of Congress Control Number: 2010917552

Printed in the United States of America

Balboa Press rev. date: 1/21/2011

Huge thank you's to:

My mom and dad, Roxy and Zarven—for loving me unconditionally, and for being a role model for what love looks like. (We all miss you Daddy!)

My sisters Cindy, Nancy, Penny, and Susie—for always believing in me, even when I didn't believe in myself. Thank you for your tireless loving advice through all of my relationship issues, and for not ever saying "oh god, there she goes again…when will she ever learn."

My kids, Ariana and Austin (I'm going to cry writing this)…for being the most beautiful, precious gifts a mom could ever ask for. I love you with all my heart and soul. Thank you for your patience, and your love. I love who each of you is becoming, and am in awe that I had something to do with it.

My angel Talia…for bringing me back to God so many years ago.

Luke…for your love and support of all that I do, and all that I am.
Brunnie…for your constant love and friendship…and for always reminding me how to be gentle with myself.
Michelle…for your support, friendship and excitement about this material!
Charlie…one of my mirrors…and one of my biggest cheerleaders…I'm still waiting to see your cartwheel!
Peter…another soul mirror…thank you for our conversations, all hours of the day and night, helping each other to remember what we know to be true.
Heather…I thank little Joanna for bringing us together. I appreciate your blunt relationship advice, always delivered lovingly, with humor. You are an inspiration to me.
Maureen…my soul-sister, for making me laugh until my stomach hurts.
My former husband Rich…thank you for being one of my best friends still. We did good, didn't we?
Heidi…another soul-sister, I'm glad we've both got shoulders for each other to lean on!

v

Susan…my other mother…lol…thank you for always checking in on me, reminding me to take care of myself.

Kathleen…for helping me to laugh at myself, and for your soulful friendship.

Steven Schwartz…my photographer…thank you for your vision. You made it fun to feel like a model for a day! I love the cover, Steve. www.stevenschwartzphotography.com.

Pam Guerrieri, of Proofed to Perfection—thank you to you and Jennifer, for your enthusiasm for this project, and for the loving way you helped to sculpt this manuscript.

To all those at Balboa Press, for working with me to bring this book to print.

Are you still with me? I feel like I'm making an acceptance speech, and the music is now starting to play. LOL

To all of my past clients, thank you for allowing me to touch your heart.

To all of you reading this…thank you for opening your heart to this book.

And last, but far from least…

To God, my source, my co-creator, my inspiration…thank you for life itself.

*I am you… you are me…we are One.*

To the reader:

There is no coincidence that you "happened" to pick up this book at this point in your life. I'm not sure of the reason, but I trust that in time it will be clear for you.

You'll notice that this book has no chapters. This dialog with God was a free-flowing conversation over a two-year time span where I had many questions about my life and about life in general. So I brought them all to God, and I let myself receive responses back.

I imagine that God speaks to each one of us in a unique way, in a way that is familiar to each of us. This written dialog happens to be the way that is most comfortable for me.

My desire…is that you are able to see yourself through my life experiences and through them come to know the compassionate, at times humorous, always loving presence I call God.

My hope…is that you will be inspired to have your own conversations with God.

My dream…is that we will all come home…to love.

From my heart to yours,

Sandy

God, you are the energy of love itself.

I allow myself to be in your presence.

Your love is here.

Let love come into my mind and my thoughts.

Right here, right now.

I trust that all is as it is meant to be.

Help me to see where I have not acted out of love.

Help me to not judge,
but to have compassion for those who have acted out of fear or anger.

Help me to recognize a perceived void within me and fill it with love,

So that I don't act from fear or lack.

You are love; you are my source…forever.

And so it is…even now.

Have you ever wondered what it would be like to have a heart-to-heart conversation with God and ask whatever you wanted without reservation?

For much of my life, it seemed that talking to God was reserved for holidays, during "grace" at dinner, an occasional church visit, and in times of crisis. During those moments of "rote prayer, confession, begging, or bargaining," I certainly didn't think that God could answer me back because God was...well, GOD!

As I look back now, I don't imagine that I was really talking *with* God but more talking *at* God. To me, God was a silent, unseen observer...like a strong parent who would perhaps nod yes or no to my requests. I'm not sure why I didn't feel strongly connected to God. Maybe I was wrapped up in my own busyness, or maybe God was busy taking care of the hungry, the poor, and the less fortunate. Maybe God *was* responding to me all along, and I just wasn't "getting it."

When I was about thirty, my journey led me to the possibility of receiving Divine Guidance from the angelic realm. I'd always liked the idea of angels and believed that they were with us. So it was then that I began writing with my angels and filled many journals of encouraging, compassionate messages of their loving wisdom that would be written through me. These messages wouldn't always tell me what to do, but they offered a comforting presence that would remind me that I wasn't alone here.

Once in a while, I'd ask my questions to God directly, but more often, I felt like I didn't want to bother him since the angels had done such a nice job intermediating. And if and when I did ask God, I hardly ever sensed a response back, though sometimes I'd feel a little more peaceful after I'd prayed. Other times though, I felt like I was just talking to the ceiling—until 1993 when a real "angel" touched my life and completely changed the course of my future in thirty-one days.

When my daughter Ariana was two and a half years old, my second daughter Talia was born. She never came home from the hospital as she was born with an extremely rare metabolic disorder that claimed her life in thirty-one days. Had anyone told me ahead of time, "Sandy, here is your journey…you'll have Ariana, then two miscarriages, then you'll have Talia, who will die at a month old, then you'll have Austin exactly a year later," I'd have told them I wasn't strong enough for that kind of journey. During Talia's short life, there were many moments I'd just lay on my bed and sob, "God, I *cannot* do this…it is too painful!"

Somehow, I began to sense God's loving, peaceful energy with me during those times of despair. During that chaotic time, when I asked heartfelt questions of God, if I was real quiet, I could sense a still, small voice in my heart that offered hope and healing to my spirit. The healing journey of Talia's life and death became my first book, *Congratulations… It's an Angel*.

In fact, it was my writing—and my connection to God and the angels—that helped me to heal, to gain clarity and understanding about my life's rocky path, and this gave me a mission to help others through loss. That journey enabled me to understand that we are truly never, ever alone and that love never dies.

In the years that followed, I opened up spiritually and began to sense Spirit around me; I would "hear" Spirit thoughts. I took classes in psychic and spiritual development, began seeing clients as a Spirit Medium, and became a certified Hypnotherapist and Bereavement Facilitator.

I would sporadically turn to God for help…usually when I felt like I had nowhere else to turn. I'm not proud of how that sounds, but it was my truth. It usually took an emotional upheaval to remind me that God was there for me, with me. Why I would wait so long to turn to God, I still don't know. In the past ten years, I went through a divorce, struggled with a substantial financial loss in a bed and breakfast investment, and lost my dad to cancer.

All were extremely difficult times. I'd reach the point of intolerable emotional pain, but when the thought of God snuck up on me, I'd remember that I wasn't alone, and there was my peace. I imagine that I am resilient at the core. But I didn't want to keep testing myself to see how resilient I was. Maybe there was a way to learn and be close to God without all the pain.

I am reminded of a recent client session where a young man came to my office so that I could connect with his dad in spirit for him. He asked me, "Sandy, can you ask my dad if God spoke to him right before he died?" (His dad had been in a coma.)

Moments later, in the stillness of that room, his dad's spirit sent these thoughts back to me: "God was speaking to me since the day I was born and never stopped. I just didn't listen."

I've decided…I want to listen.

*Little one, ask and you shall receive.*

Sometimes life has something in store for you that you could never imagine. This particular Christmas, as has happened in other years, I didn't make time to send out Christmas cards. There was too much on my plate with work, shopping, and everything else that goes along with the holiday season. I felt too much pressure to snap a cute picture of the kids, get my list together, and so on. I let it all go.

So, I bought some New Year's cards to send out to friends and family instead. I thought I'd include a letter sharing what I'd wish for them in the new year. I planned to write about how a new year can symbolize new beginnings, growth, letting go of the old, and making room for the new.

I shared this idea with a friend of mine, and he mentioned a Japanese tradition of sending a brand new dollar bill with each card…to signify a brand new beginning. Such great intentions—what a fun project this would be!

On the morning of December 26, I had the house to myself since my kids were at their dad's house. Sitting down at my laptop to create the letter, I first wanted to connect with God to feel some inspiration. I started out by asking one simple question to put me into a place where I'd feel connected to my heart, thinking that it would then help me to offer wisdom in the letter. I began with one question, and I never imagined the dialog that would follow…

*December 26*

God, what should I do with the new year?

*First of all…start by taking out the "should." There is no "should."*

I am surprised by how quickly I discern a response. And I'm sensing that I'm not going to get away with any unclear words. So let me start over. God, what **shall** I do with this new year?

*Nice try, Sandy, but you're still in the "doing" mindset.*

But I need to do something with this upcoming year. How could I just do "nothing"? Isn't that why we set all those New Year's resolutions that never really get met—to feel like we're going to do something different with the next year?

*And do they work?*

For me, no, but at least I pacify that part of me that feels guilty for not setting a goal.

*You've done so much. You've accomplished much. How about resting… just for a little bit? I'm tired just watching you.*

Note to self: I like God's sense of humor.

*How about this—try "being" this year.*

5

Being what?

*Being nothing more than who you already are.*

Who I already am? Who am I? I feel like I'm playing a game of twenty questions. Who am I? Am I bigger than a breadbox? (Actually, the way I've been eating lately, I can already answer that one!)

*Note to Self: I like Sandy's sense of humor; she amuses herself well.*

I'm sorry, God. I'll be serious.

*No, please don't be. You've already done that well enough.*

So, who shall I be? I'm already a mom, a daughter, a sister, a friend, an author, a Spirit medium…who do you want me to be?

*You.*

I feel like I'm in the "Who's On First" scenario! You win, but I have no idea where this is going.

*That's a good sign—to not know where something is going. But that is where many people let fear come in. So many of you hold onto the energy of "I need to know what's going to happen"…with relationships, with finances, with careers. You take the fun out of it. It's all a game, and the only rules are the ones you believe in. But many of you believe in fear-based rules: if you don't do this, you won't be able to pass go and collect your $200. Stop playing monopoly. Lighten up. End this game of "man-opoly"—this game of trying to capture and gain and compete for who has more, who is more. Stop the nonsense. You're making it all up, and it's not why you're here.*

So why are we here?

*Are you sure you want to know?*

Um....yes.

*You are here to be...me.*

To be you?

*Yes, to be me.*

I thought you just said you wanted me to be me. Now you're saying you want me to be you. I'm confused.

*Because I am you, you are me, and we are one.*

Oh, God, people aren't going to accept this. I can hear them now. Who do you think you are, to say that we are here to be God?

*So, let them know that ME stands for Master Emerging. If they can't accept that they are here to be God in physical form, let them know that there is a master within them that wants to emerge. You have been aware of this for quite some time, little one, but your resistance and doubt overshadows it at times. You know this in your heart, and it will resonate with the hearts of those who can hear. Those that cannot may call you a heretic, a blasphemer, a false prophet. Those are not my words. Those are from fear...the place that holds no light.*

*Ask them if their fearful way of being has worked for them. How is it bringing in more light, more love to the world? How is it bringing healing to the many hearts (starting with their own) that are calling out for love? Fear cannot do that. Love/God can. Only love is real. The rest is of the imagination, or image-in-nation. Your nations hold images of war, and that is what they experience. Your nations hold images of lack, and that is what they experience. Perhaps more will be ready to hold images of peace and love, but I tell you this: it must start within their hearts first. It begins with the one heart. One heart...one mind...*

What? The individual heart, the individual mind?

*You could say that, but it is more the one heart...one mind...of God. You all are created of it...share it still...but many have separated themselves from it. It is time to come home, to be conscious of it. Bring awareness to the one heart—one mind of God—where all things are possible, where fear does not exist.*

I have to laugh because I really sat down at my laptop this morning to compose a New Year's letter to friends and family...and I didn't expect you to show up! I don't mean any disrespect by that. It just surprised me, that's all!

*And I was here this morning, and I didn't expect you to show up. I am not disrespecting you either, Sandy. It surprised me because you so often try to do this work all by yourself. I'm here for you always. I was contemplating composing a letter to my friends and family (every human on the planet) and you showed up—ready and willing to be guided.*

But you're God. How could you be surprised? Don't you know everything? Don't you know when we're hurting...or confused? I had a client recently who shared the stories of all the painful challenges in her life. She said to me, "What was God thinking?!" So, may I ask? What are you thinking?

*Very simply...love. Always. In all ways.*

So, for us to be more like you, we will need to think about love more?

*Yes...or rather, think from love more.*

OOH, that may be so difficult, God. Such hurt exists in people's hearts here.

*And that is how they are creating their lives—from hurt, from pain. It doesn't need to be that way, and you will be my messenger. You are one of many who are willing to get the word out. Be my voice here, Sandy.*

I can already feel fear in my gut.

*Is that from me?*

No, it's from me. I know this has been coming for quite some time now. I give in; I surrender. I am willing to be your voice here. Oh, God, I hope I get the translation right.

*You make me smile...so silly. Watch the fear and let it pass. It's not from me.*

Then where is it from?

*It is from your old beliefs that have told you that you aren't enough, but you are...you all are.*

So what are we going to talk about? Where do we start? I feel a little like Neale Donald Walsch, author of "Conversations with God", when he first started having his conversations with you. Though, I'm very grateful that I didn't have to be down and out on the street, like he did, to wake up. I've been waking up slowly for the last fifteen years. I guess I kept hitting the snooze button, huh?

*Like so many do, Sandy, like so many do. Trust. This dialog will reach many and will melt the walls around their hearts. Some of what I am going to give to you will feel familiar...some of it will be new to you. Let go of how you think it should be.*

Alrighty then, I guess I'm hired for the job? And I didn't even have to get out of my pajamas for this! Thanks, God. I'm excited about this; it's something that's been in my heart for a long, long time...writing another book, with you. Hey, do you like the *Little Seed of Hope* book? It was written through me in about twenty minutes on the plane to Sedona in May. You're in it!

*Who do you think gave it to you?*

Ha ha...I get it. Thanks, I love the concept; I think others will too. So now what?

*Let's start at the beginning...*

Rut roh, (I say in my best Scooby Doo voice), the beginning? I hate history. You should know that. It's so boring to me. And I don't like watching the news either. The images are too depressing. Those images stick in people's minds with all the negativity that is shown. My sisters have teased me about not knowing what is going on in the world, but what is more important to me is what is going on in people's hearts.

*What is going on in their hearts becomes what is going on in the world. Let me repeat that...what is going on in their hearts becomes what is going on in the world. And that is what this is all about...for that is the beginning I was referring to. The beginning, the middle, and the end are the same; it is the journey back to the heart...the journey back to love.*

Hey, can we call this *What Was God Thinking*? I like that title. Oh wait! Oh my God...*The Journey Back to the Heart* was my working title of Talia's book before I was inspired to call it *Congratulations...It's an Angel*. Were you preparing me back then? Oops, I'm jumping ahead, aren't I? I am just excited about this. It must be my ADD mind.

*Watch how you label yourself, Sandy. You've claimed it, but is that a loving way to describe your mind?*

No, but I joke about it all the time.

*Don't do it; it hurts you and keeps you in that mindset. You've got a brilliant, creative mind. Affirm that...notice the difference in how it feels.*

I have a brilliant, creative mind; ooh, it feels like something is expanding. But, God, I don't want this to be about me. Will people want to read this?

*Sandy, you've always had a way of letting your vulnerability be seen, and so many have told you that they can identify with the path you're on. They can see themselves through your writings. So let that go...and trust.*

God, hold on a second. I need to make some tea. This is so fun! Do you mind that I'm asking you to wait?

*Everyone asks me to wait; they just don't know they're doing it. They ask me to wait anytime they let fear in...when they forget that love is present. So you could say I've been in a holding pattern...just waiting for people to be ready. Waiting for you to make some tea is nothing.*

God, you're very funny, you know.

*So are you, and that is why this is working now. You wanted to write a funny book. You just didn't imagine I'd be part of it.*

No, I didn't. Okay, I can't lie. I'm not making tea; I'm making some chai. Why do I feel like I needed to tell you that? I'm laughing to myself— as if it matters—tea or chai, who cares? This is so fun! I'll be right back... don't go anywhere!

*That's what I've been trying to tell you all: don't go anywhere...I'm here for you. Go make your chai.*

~~~~~~

I'm back; are you still here? I have to laugh...because it's not like you have anywhere else to go, right? Or do you?

*Sandy, there is no place...no time...just now. There is nowhere else for me to go—nowhere. And that is where you are—nowhere.*

Is that a good thing?

*What do you think?*

I know in my heart the feeling that I'm going nowhere can be scary.

*Look at the word differently...nowhere...now-here.*

That's entirely different then. Being now-here is very peaceful.

*And which is from love?*

Being now-here. Going nowhere has fear attached to it. Hey, God, don't we need a structure for this book? I mean, won't people need to know what they'll get from this book: ten secrets...nine ways...eight ideas...seven ladies dancing...six geese a laying...

*Five golden rings...that was my favorite line. Think about it. The golden ring is all about love. No beginning...no end...like life, death, life again, death again. So, do you want to have structure? This is your book.*

You're asking me? But you're God! I thought this was your book.

*We are one, Sandy. Remember you are learning how to be me.*

I don't always like making decisions about big stuff because I can see it from many angels. Ha ha...I just wrote many angels. I meant to say angles.

*You had it right the first time. You do have an ability to see decisions from many perspectives, but you fear that you'll make a decision that is wrong. At some point, you'll see that you cannot. Any decision that a person chooses, is made because on a soul level that person needed to experience the lessons that come with that path of choice.*

So, can we start with death and how we can help people see it differently?

*How about we start with life and help people see it differently. The approach to life and death are truly the same. One can approach it with fear and trepidation or with joy and peace—with positive expectancy.*

Go ahead; you're the boss.

*You're silly.*

So about life, where do we start?

*At the beginning, which some will assume is birth. But birth is not really the beginning—merely the beginning of physical form…of spirit taking human form. There really is no beginning; like your breath, it is one continuous flow… sometimes the breath goes in…sometimes it goes out, but it is still breath, no? Just like the process of birth and death…sometimes your spirit enters the body, and sometimes it exits the body. You are always energy.*

I like that analogy; you're good!

*But many people try and compartmentalize birth and death to help them to understand it. That's why you try to compartmentalize anything…to try to understand it. But in the process, you lose the essence of the bigger picture. So, let's look at the idea of no-birth, no-death, but a continuation of breath. See how that word* breath *is actually a combination of birth/death—bir…eath— breath…one continuous cycle for the purpose of experiencing and expressing love. Breathing in love, breathing out love. Bringing love in…letting love out. How simple, yet so hard for so many. So, let's look at it. The process of birth can be painful and traumatic…*

I know. We were just talking about that at our family gathering yesterday. My mother told us how painful a couple of my sisters' births were. She said I was easy!

*As the soul enters the body, it can be traumatic for the mom and for the baby. If there is fear present, the soul is aware of it, but it knows ahead of time. Let me take you one step further back. We have conversations, you know, your soul and I before your spirit decides to take the journey back into its body. We discuss the lessons, opportunities, and experiences that the lifetime would have for you (the soul). What makes me smile is the enthusiasm that you share—the willingness to go into the body to help others…in the script of their lives…to play the "good" guy, the "bad" guy, the one who won't forgive, the one who loves. It is all done in a spirit of love. But when you enter the world of illusion, you forget the rules of spirit and adopt the rules of the world. There is but one rule of spirit that you are sent with. Love.*

But what about people who do bad things? People who commit crimes? People who are mean? Did they veer off course so far that they forgot about love?

*Here's where you all veer off course—even those who commit crimes. They have chosen to play that role this time in the body. You have all played it before but have most likely forgotten. You may be in a lifetime of a healer now, but in another life, you may have hurt others. You sense that yourself, Sandy, that many who come to you for healing are those that you may have hurt in another lifetime. All people come back again to balance the energy…to be a force for good, for light in the world. You all do that; you keep entering and exiting the body like getting on a roller coaster again and again…because the ride can be fun. My "job" is to help you return to love…*

In thought, in word, in deed…?

*Indeed!*

Wait…go back a second. You said that the ride can be fun. God, what about all the people who are hurting, who are in grief, who are in fear? This ride is not fun to them nor would I want to suggest that they are supposed to be having fun…not in the throes of their pain.

*Nor am I…what I am suggesting is that we look at what keeps people in pain. Deal?*

Now you sound like Howie Mandell…deal or no deal? Okay, deal!

*Sandy, I think we may need a little structure here. You do have a beautifully creative mind, which is very active. Take a deep breath, and let's agree that this book will be about helping people return to their hearts. This book will help them look at what keeps them in pain in life through relationships, through money, through work, through death. Sound fair?*

Sounds like a plan.

*You were created out of love. You live with love; you die with love, but many of you have no idea of that. You see pain all around you. You feel the injustices of the world and wonder, "Where is God?" in it all? I am in your hearts, but you have forgotten to look there. It is often the last place you go because you have strongly identified with the mind. That is not a bad thing, but you have identified with the mind of the world—not the mind of God. The mind of the world holds fear. The mind of God is love. People make choices every day, but many do it from fear. It is time to stop. Literally, stop the mind chatter. Stop the fearful movie that you replay repeatedly.*

*You do have that choice you know. To choose higher. Choose higher thoughts. Choose higher visions. Choose higher words. Choose higher actions. With regard to life, it is not a coincidence that you are with your family of origin…though many of you question that. You all are waking up to the idea that the soul comes into physical form so you can experience yourself as me… masters emerging.*

God, what about people who have been abused? Born into homes where there was no love present…why would they choose that on a soul level? How could they possibly know about love when all they knew was pain?

*To remember love…to understand forgiveness…to practice compassion… to find their way back to their hearts.*

Isn't that a cruel way for them to learn?

*Some would think so, but there are many paths back to the heart; some will choose a difficult one. Some have already been there and will choose a lighter journey.*

Why on earth would anyone choose a difficult life path? To me, that would be like going through labor with no epidural! Ouch, ouch, ouch!

*But some do, Sandy, for the experience of it, knowing that the pain will not last, knowing that when they have that beautiful baby in their arms, the thoughts of pain are but a memory.*
*The same is true with life. On a soul level, the pain that many go through is like labor pain…as they use their experiences to recreate themselves anew. Some go through life feeling every bit of pain…hard, hard pain…to help them to learn. One needs not to be in pain to learn. Let me say that again for those who didn't get it…**one needs not to be in pain to learn**. Life will be as painful as you allow it to be. Others go through life numbing themselves so they won't feel their pain. And some will go through life with an awareness that I am with them and feel the peace that accompanies that. It's a choice…all of it. And you can choose differently in every moment.*

We don't always remember that we have a choice. We've become creatures of habit and are sometimes on autopilot. We've sort of gotten used to being in pain, being comfortably uncomfortable.

*Yes, that's true, but what you don't realize is that when you choose to remember love, the pain can become a distant memory. But many have unconsciously chosen to hold on to it, hitting rewind and replay. But we are getting ahead of ourselves. We will talk more about that in a little bit when we talk about holding on to pain.*

God, so here is the million-dollar question: What the heck is this thing called love anyway?

*What is it to you, little one?*

I used to think it was something you felt. But now I wonder if it is that, but more. That when you feel it, you act from it. I imagine it can be different things: appreciation, peace, acceptance…

*Good, go on.*

Joy, wisdom, compassion…grace? Is that right?

*All wonderful descriptions of all that is.*

God, I have to take a break. My head is so full right now. I think I have to do something different like clean the house for a little bit. You don't mind, do you?

*I'm here for you always…in all ways…for always.*

~ ~ ~ ~ ~ ~ ~

I'm back. Where would you like to start?

*Let's talk about love, for that is what this book is about, remembering love in every part of life and death.*
*Think back to your experiences at the conference you attended last month. Many of the people there called each other "love" (for example, "How are you, love?"). How you loved that because it felt like they reached inside your soul and saw you for who you really are.*

Yes, and I said I wanted to start calling people "love." "Hi, love…" "You look good today, love!" I love how that sounds—sounds very, well, loving.

*Because it is.*

I felt like I was more expansive there…no boundaries, no fear. Actually, there was some fear because I was beginning to feel attached to someone there. Can we talk about attachments?

*Sure, how do you see attachments in relationships?*

15

You ask good questions, God. I see attachments as coming from… hmm…not love, but fear. When someone impacts my life in a positive way, I have had a tendency to think that they are the source of my happiness or joy…that without them, my happiness would not be the same, that I would not be complete. So I attach myself to their energy.

*And what happens then?*

Then I decide how they need to be there for me, which as I write this sounds so silly, but it is how I've approached relationships in the past. When I've formed an attachment and the other person has decided to choose differently, then I have been hurt.

*Is your attachment real? Do you attach to them with a rope?*

No, it is in my mind.

*So, it is an illusion that you are attached to them.*

Yes, but it feels so real.

*As most illusions do. So how are you attached to them? Through love… or fear?*

Hmm…it must be through fear; yes, through fear, and that's my final answer! Am I right?

*Yes. Love does not attach. Love simply is. Fear tries to attach for the reasons you so love-ly put. Fear tries to tell you that you are less without that person. Fear says that you are more complete with them. Though you think that other people and other things are your source of happiness, you will come to know that nothing truly sources you other than me. Attachments are a source of pain. Notice what has been happening to you lately as you release any attachments that you are aware of.*

I feel peace.

*Which is from love or fear?*

Love.

*Good, you're getting it.*

So why do we hold on to fear in relationships?

*You fear loss. At the root of it is a fear of loss. At the core of it is a sense of missing me and the unconditional love from Home. I have never left you and you are now remembering how to return to love...to the energy of Home.*

*Fear is the absence of me...of love. When love is present, fear is not. When truth is present, fear is not. When God is present, fear is not. When you are present, fear is not.*

Help me out with that last one. "When you are present, fear is not."

*Many are not present in the moment, Sandy. You have known that firsthand. It is only recently that you are learning to be present in a relationship without seeing your beloved through the eyes of your wounds and without worrying about where it is headed, but simply being in the presence of loving thought, in the present moment, and allowing the present moment to create the future that your heart desires.*

*In many relationships, people are not present, and fear often stems from fearful images from the past that you repeatedly play over and over again in your mind, right? Times when people have left you or lied to you or withheld love from you. In essence, many people are not fully present in relationships. They relive their past, rehash an old wound from their past, trying to hold another accountable for their pain. It won't ever work that way. One needs to be accountable for their wounds and let love heal them. It is then that you will be able to be fully present in a relationship.*

*There is more to it. Relationships that are fully present are open, honest, and reflect love. Love in its purest form does not hold another back from being all that they are created to be. Many have not understood what love is. They have had a misunderstanding...if they experienced pain as a child, they began to think that love hurts. Love doesn't hurt. It heals. If it hurts, it is not love. It is fear. If it hurts, it may be an illusion that is being destroyed, so that love may enter in another form.*

Wow, that's a lot, but it makes sense...I need a break! Don't you ever get tired from all this wisdom?

*No, but so many of you get tired from all the fear. You are becoming weary from all the fear, and soon, you will tire of all the fear and return to love. That is why we are writing this book. Go, take a break. I am here for you always... in all ways...for always.*

*December 27*

Good morning, God. I've got my tea. I joked with a friend this morning that I hoped you'd be back from Dunkin Donuts and ready to write. This is real, isn't it?

*Good morning to you, little one. And I joked with Archangel Michael this morning that I hoped you'd already gotten your tea and would be ready to write this morning. And what is behind the question of "this is real, isn't it?"?*

I just never imagined writing a dialog like this with you. You speak my language. I understand you.

*Sandy, I speak to each of you, yet you will each "hear" me differently in a language that you can relate to. Some think that I only spoke through the Bible, so that is how they hear my words. Some think I speak in harsh tones, reprimanding them when they "sin." But know this: for all, my language is the same; it is the language of love. How each person hears it may differ, and that is okay..*

So you don't mind when we joke, do you? You know I love you and I love this process.

*No, I don't mind when you joke, but sometimes jokes can hurt others, and that hurts all. Remember the saying "all for one, and one for all?" I'd rather you think of it as "all is one, and one is all." What that means is that when you hurt one, you hurt all. When you love one, you love all.*

18

And when we hurt another, we really hurt ourselves?

*There really is no difference, little one. You wouldn't be able to love another without loving yourself first. You cannot hurt another without hurting yourself first. You cannot give what you don't have. When you no longer have hurt, you no longer hurt others. You know how hard it is for you to be around people who gossip or complain about others? But in your not-so-long-ago life, you did that yourself, no?*

Yes, I did. It was a mindset I was in years ago, and I'm not proud of it. It's where I was at that point of my life, mostly complaining about relationships but feeling powerless to change anything.

*Was it powerlessness or was it fear?*

It was fear, but isn't that the same thing?

*Sort of…but the idea of powerlessness stems from fear. All emotions stem from either love or fear. And even though fear is not real, many make it to be so real in their minds. And even though love is very real, many fear it because of old fear. It is a vicious cycle they are in.*

*But you don't complain as much nor do you gossip anymore, do you? Because of how you have chosen to heal and grow, it's not in you to do that.*

No, I really don't. It hurts my heart to be around people who gossip.

*Look at what you just wrote…*

What? That it hurts my heart to be around people who gossip?

*Yes. Do you know why?*

No.

*You feel the energy that they emit. The energy of the words that are used when people complain, gossip, hate, and so on is a far different energy than the words of love. And so when that energy is released, it is sent to the universe in waves and adds to the negativity that is in your world. Yes, the effects can be felt, consciously or not. So you see that when you hold negativity in your heart, it truly does affect your world.*

*The same is true for loving words; the energy vibration is much higher and holds healing with it, so even when you love your dog, that love you send him is felt by more than him.*

*My hope is that more people awaken to these concepts of how they are able to heal or harm by their thoughts, words, and actions. For there really is just a flow…thoughts become words, words become actions…all powerful tools that have the potential to heal.*

It's hard, when you're in it, to see it. I feel like I was blind at one point to much of what we're talking about because I was in such drama and chaos. It was so difficult to see any wisdom when I was in the drama. Can we talk about drama and chaos?

*Oh, the drama that you all create. We hold you and are here for you even when you are in a state of forgetfulness…that's all it really is.*

Wow, you make it seem so simple; drama is JUST forgetfulness? How come it's so hard to be in it and to remember that we're in it?

*Are you ready for this?*

Uh oh, I think so…

*Because some people love the drama, love the chaos, and are not fully aware that they love it…because it makes them feel more alive. On some level, they have gleaned attention when they have had dramatic moments, and perhaps they came to believe that the only way they could garner more attention was to create drama. No judgment…just a path of learning for them. For others, they don't know any other way to create in life. They've held the energy of "victim," which permeates every part of their lives.*

I know that to be true. It's hard for me to be around victim energy.

*Don't judge it, dear one; you have played the victim in other lifetimes…oh, did you play it well! But you didn't come into this lifetime to play the victim.*
*So, for those who carry the energy of victim, they've created an energetic field around them of thoughts and ideas of how life is…for them. They've agreed to the idea that they are victims. On a soul level, they signed up for it…to work through the heaviness of it. They need not to be stuck in it forever. For anyone who chooses to remember love, no matter what the situation or lesson, as soon as love hits, the energy is transformed. This is an important concept that I don't want to gloss over.*

Okay. So are you saying that illness, disease, lack, guilt, etc. for all the "yucky"…

*Watch how you're judging those to be "bad." As soon as you judge something, you keep yourself attached to it through fear. Sandy, these are all simply ideas that hold the potential to bring you back to love.*

So, are you saying that when someone brings love to the parts of themselves that may have been victimized, filled with guilt, or shamed, that the illness or disease will go away? It sounds too simple, though a part of me knows this to be true.

*In Spirit, there is no illness, dis-ease, guilt, shame, etc. There is only love. In the world that you all have created, you have experiences other than love. Sometimes the illness is needed to help another learn compassion, selflessness, caring…and not just for the one agreeing to the illness.*

So, it could be that other family members are meant to learn and grow through it as well?

*All is one, and one is all; they each will have an opportunity to remember love through it. For those that do, there will be peace. For those that don't, they won't feel the peace that is within them already.*

Wait, go back. So if one remembers love during an illness, they'll feel peace, but will they still have the illness?

*If there are other reasons for them to hold it, yes. But peace, even in the midst of an illness, is a higher state of consciousness than lack of peace without an illness. Many of you hold on to the idea that healthy is better than sick, living is better than dying. I say to you that peace and love are the highest choices, regardless of what the surroundings look like. Do not judge sickness; do not judge death: neither of those is "bad." They are just experiences of energy transformation.*

Ooh, there's a lot to this, and I can feel my resistance to putting this out there.

*That's alright. What is your resistance?*

That it's so different, telling people that sickness and death are not "bad." Our whole society is built on trying not to get sick, trying not to die, trying not to age, or trying not to look older. So there is a pill for this, a pill for that—liposuction, plastic surgery.

*And how does that help people to look within their hearts to find the remembrance of love?*

I'm not sure that it does; it masks pain, conceals symptoms, gives the quick fix that people look for.

*Let me say this: all of those things are not bad either. Sandy, nothing is "bad" when love is present.*

God, why are we so afraid of death? I think since Talia died I don't see death as a bad thing anymore.

*It's not.*

But why are so many here frightened by it?

*Because many think that death is the end, that there will be judgment, that this is the one chance you get around the merry-go-round of life. To address that, death is not the end; there is no judgment other than what you're already holding yourself in, and this is not your one shot at it. If you really knew that, you'd take yourself to another level of peace instantaneously.*

*You have been sensing that your role is to help people see death differently. In your work with connecting with Spirit, you've been given much opportunity to understand death differently, and yes, it is time to share more of what you have come to understand. Don't worry; I'll help you if you get stuck. Look to some of your writing in the past around death. As you help others to look at their fear of death, they will also begin to look at their fear of life; it is one and the same.*

Thank you, God.

*You are most welcome.*

*December 28*

Good morning, God, I only have a few minutes this morning because I start early with clients….one at seven thirty and one at nine, then off to Ariana's basketball tournament.

*You don't normally schedule clients on Thursdays, do you?*

No, I don't, but these people couldn't make it any other time. I wanted to accommodate them.

*Can we look at the word* accommodate*?*

Sure, but I have to tell you that I really don't know where you're going with this. I'm already seeing the word *commode* in it. Please tell me that it has nothing to do with a toilet!

*You are funny so early this morning and quick too, Sandy—just something for you to notice. Accommodating another is not a bad thing unless it makes all your other plans "go down the toilet," which again is not a bad thing…unless you are doing it out of a "should," which then can lead you to resentment. Remember that nothing is bad…just watch your reasons for doing what you do. Especially since you tend to put others first at the expense of being authentic with yourself in your effort to not disappoint another, in an attempt to please. You're not alone there; many do that. But it takes you away from your true nature, which is to love yourself and others.*

*Ready for this too? When you accommodate and accommodate, you end up feeling like that which goes down the toilet.*

Oh, God, that's gross. I don't know if I'm going to keep that in. Ew. Okay, thanks, I will be more aware of that. But what I wanted to really ask you about this morning, since I didn't have much time, was this idea that I hold about being in "hurry-up" mode, of trying to fit stuff in.

*And you're trying to hurry up and fit it in this morning, right? Relax, little one, there really is no concept of time, other than what you have decided that it means. It has run you and your life for some time and has given you this hurry-up mentality…not just with your children, but in relationships, in your career, in buying your home. It has been with you; so let's look at it, shall we?*

Sure. I think it's tied to this idea of making sure it's the "right" relationship, the right career move, the right home…and being afraid that if I don't get it right, then someone else will come and take the opportunity, that I'll have missed my chance at happiness, at that "right" thing that comes in quickly and will go away quickly if I don't hurry up and make a move. Oh, I know that this sounds silly, but it is what is in my mind.

*So, let's start slowly. Breathe first, little one. There's no hurry to this answer even if you have to go get ready to leave for the office. There's a little thread of worry in your mind that if you don't "hurry up" and get this answer, then you won't get it later when you resume this writing.*

You are in my head, aren't you? That's exactly what I'm thinking!

*Dearest little one, I am not only in your head, I am in every cell within you. I am you, you are me, and we are one. Breathe. I am here with you always.*

Thank you, I feel more peaceful, and I really do have to go take a shower now. You're good, God; I trust you. I'll be back later this afternoon, okay? Much love to you.

*Back at you, Sandy. And I didn't do this to test you…I don't throw down tests to see if you'll pass or fail. Would love do that? You are being given an opportunity to relax into what would've held fear for you. No test, no grade… just experience. Witness it. Now go shower.*

~~~~~

Hey God, I'm back; my client sessions went well. I worked with a mom and her three young kids—their father died ten months ago. Those sessions always pull at my heart. I can't imagine what they're going through.

*They'll be alright, Sandy; you were there for them, and they will be okay. We hold them in love, in light, in remembrance of truth...that death is not the end. You conveyed that well for them...thank you for that.*

You're welcome. So can we talk about this hurry-up mentality? Because here we go again...I have to leave in fifteen minutes for Ari's basketball tournament.

*Relax, little one. Actually, why don't you go take a break and redo that load of laundry that has been on your mind all day?*

You mean the one that is in the washer...that I've already washed three times because I keep forgetting it's there? Oh, God, now everyone will know...it's true though. I've rewashed this same load of laundry three times in a row because every time I remember to put it in the dryer, it's gotten smelly because it waited a few days, so I re-wash it! This is a first for me...four times! Ugh! Please tell me that I'm not the only one that does this.

*Sandy, don't worry; you just enamored more readers. You are not alone, I guarantee you. Go do the wash. I'll be here now and later because it is all the same to me.*

*I am here for you always, in all ways, for always.*

*December 30*

Hey, God, I finally got that load of laundry complete! Yay! It's never-ending. I took the kids to the mall yesterday, met with a couple clients, and was a guest on the FUN 107 radio show yesterday morning. The format is called "Free Fortune Friday," where people call in to get a mini reading. I'm supposed to connect with Spirit for them on the phone.

I found that people so wanted me to tell them what's going to happen. What's going to happen in their relationships? Is he the one? Should I stay...should I go...will he change...can I trust him? Or with finances, they want to know: will it get better? Will I ever get out of debt? Should I buy this house or should I wait? So many are in a mode of "I need to know...someone tell me what's going to happen!" I've been there and even still feel like that once in a while.

*So what did you tell the listeners?*

Oh, God, I told them that there isn't just one path, one potential for us. That there are many potentials that we can experience. And that each thought that we hold activates a different set of potentials. That's right, isn't it?

*It is; there is a blueprint for your life, but how you steer through it leaves lots of room for your thoughts, and decisions based on those thoughts influence the direction of how you navigate through the blueprint. Just like your laundry, there are many ways to do it: you can wash that load of laundry once or many times; the end result is the same, no?*

Ha ha…yes, but I don't want to keep repeating the same thing in my life just to get to the end.

*So think of why you had to keep rewashing the laundry.*

Are you serious? Why do we keep talking about the laundry? I thought it was just silliness on my part.

*Is it? Think of why you had to keep rewashing the laundry, Sandy.*

Because I forgot it was there, because I got busy, because I got distracted. We're not really talking about laundry here, are we? This applies to life… wow. When I get busy, forgetful, distracted, I keep redoing things.

*Yes, little one…there is no judgment here…just an opportunity to learn from it. The laundry was moved to the back of your mind and so then forgotten about. I have been moved to the back of so many minds and forgotten about; that is partly why so many suffer. It does not affect me when people forget me—it affects them. Think about how busyness, distraction, and forgetfulness drain you of energy in daily life.*

We can be so busy that we forget to take time to fill ourselves with love, and we experience emptiness, which is when, for me, doubt comes in. We can be so distracted, not being able to hear your thoughts, and we experience fear. We can forget that you are with us every step of the way, and we experience worry. We forget that this universe is abundant and experience lack.

*Like forgetting about the laundry—the laundry was there all the time.*

Yes, and I'm sensing there's more to it.

*Always can be…*

I do get so busy sometimes that I feel out of sync with what is truly important here, taking care of the little things in life, spending more quality time with my parents and my kids…and even our dog, Mikey. I know when it's happening I don't always stop myself from the craziness though. And sometimes when I do stop, I'll feel such a craving to cook, to clean, to nest, to organize paperwork, to finish laundry…taking care of those important things fills some place within me.

*It is about being present, Sandy, which brings us to the hurry-up syndrome that we started talking about the other day—the hurry-up feeling that takes you out of the moment. We can look at that.*

Alright, but I can't right now because now I have to go get ready to take Ari to basketball and go see a couple clients. I'll be back...I promise.

*I'll be here...I promise.*

~~~~~

I'm back, God. It's quiet here; the kids are with Rich tonight. A friend of mine asked me if I had a date tonight. I didn't want to tell him that yes, I did—a date with God. Not that you are a last choice...

*Sandy, why do you think you are alone in your house tonight?*

Because I wasn't invited anywhere?

*But you were.*

Actually, you're right. A couple people asked if I'd like to go out tonight, but nothing felt like it was inviting enough to make me want to go out.

*Because there was another reason.*

Okay, I give up.

*To be here in this moment. Listen...it's silent. You don't get that often. What do you hear?*

I hear Mikey running around upstairs; I hear the other computer humming. Wait, is that supposed to be happening? I might have to call Timmy to come and look at the computer. Sorry...my thoughts wandered.

*Look around you. What do you see?*

I see the fire in the fireplace, (which I think this gas fireplace was one of the best purchases I've ever made). I see this computer screen, the water bottle on the table beside me, the *Talladega Nights* DVD box. Where are we going with this? I feel like I'm playing "I spy with my little eye..."—sorry, I know you have a point here, but I'm not exactly sure what it is.

*What do you feel physically?*

My back is a little sore; actually, my shoulders are tense from typing this way on the laptop…

*What do you feel emotionally?*

Hmm…right now, I feel truly peaceful. Why do you ask?

*Because this little exercise was to help you bring your senses into the moment; it is the present moment that holds peace. You felt a little fear earlier this afternoon, right?*

Yes, but I don't really want to go into that right now.

*Don't worry, I won't reveal what it was about, but you may want to see how you were not present in the moment. Were you?*

No, I wasn't at all. I was worried about a guy I dated a few times, who I really felt a connection with. I hadn't heard from him…and I know I allowed my worry to cloud my moments. I felt it around my heart and in my throat.

*You allowed your fear to not only come into your present moment, but what you were really afraid of was that your future would be altered…you created a picture that held fear because of attachments.*

I thought we were going to talk about the hurry-up syndrome?

*It's all part of it, little one. You wanting to hear from your friend stemmed from that energy. "If he doesn't hurry up and call me…then…then…" Then what?*

Then I'd be mad…and hurt. If I was going to be hurt, then I'd rather know now and get it out of the way. It's the not knowing that I dislike the most. Not knowing under which circumstance or when we may have to feel pain can be scary.

*Did you know what you were going to have to feel when your daughter Talia was born?*

No, and I've said often that the first week and a half of her life when we didn't know if she would live was the hardest because we didn't know what to prepare for. Once they told us she was going to die, I could wrap

29

my little mind around the concept and start the grieving process. In the not knowing, you don't know what you're going to have to feel…and you don't know how deeply you'll have to feel it…

*Looking back now, you still understand that even when Talia was taken off the respirator and you were told that she would probably live twelve to twenty-four hours, that it was still a challenge because she made it past the twenty-four hours. She lived for another week. My point is that no matter how you prepare, it is still hard—no matter what. You thought you were bracing yourself for her death…yet there is no way to protect yourself from the pain of it. I suggest to all to try to not prepare for pain…to not brace yourself for it… but to em-brace it…yes, embrace it to let yourself move into it…softly, feeling it and letting yourself dance with it.*

Oh, God, how can you say that? Embrace the pain? Dance with the pain?

*Little one, people's fear of pain is quite often much worse than the pain itself. It sets the mind up for battle. When one is in fight mode, one resists the process of what is trying to be moved through them. To embrace it all is to allow the energy to continue to move. To dance with it is to learn that it can be a powerful teacher, and you are the student.*

God, I need a break. I'm going to go make a salad for dinner…I'll be right back.

*I'll be here…or there…or wherever you are.*

*December 31*

God, I had my salad last night and ended up watching a *Jerry Seinfeld* DVD instead. My head was too full to write…I hope you don't mind.

*Sandy, so many think I get upset when they don't connect with me. The truth is that you could never NOT be connected with me…though so many don't feel it and wonder if I am upset with them. I am you, you are me, and we are one. I am here for you whenever you are ready. I am with you always.*

Thank you, God. I want to be more like you…in so many ways. I want to be able to move through all challenges easily, smoothly, without getting frustrated, irritated, and impatient. I want to love more.

*But you are learning, little one, and you are finding yourself spending less and less time in those places of frustration, irritation, and impatience. Do you see that?*

Yes, but I still feel so human at times.

*Sandy, you are funny; that's because you still are, little one. Go easy on yourself. Many judge themselves so harshly because they think they should be further along than they are. Please tell them to release the judgment; it holds them back and keeps them stuck there. You are all doing the best with the tools you have. Relax and remember to enjoy this journey.*

Thanks. I find it hard to relax sometimes because…here it is again… that feeling of wanting to hurry up and "be there."

*Be where? Where is "there"?*

Ha ha…good question. Hmm….be where? Where am I hurrying to be? Well, lately, I guess I feel like I'm in a hurry to be in a relationship.

*But you are in a relationship…with many men…as friends.*

I know, but I mean in a long-term committed relationship with a man who loves me as much as I love him. I miss that.

*What do you imagine it would bring you that is not in your life now?*

It would bring the feeling of not having to look anymore…not having to wonder anymore when it will happen, with whom it will be, and so on.

*You've just identified what it would not bring you, but what would it bring to you? Follow that along; many reading this will identify with what you're going through.*

I guess it would bring me more peace…though I know what you're going to say…

*Yes, you do.*

That I can have peace with or without being in a relationship. I already know that, and I already do have peace much of the time. But I think there is a part of me that has decided that it is better to be in a relationship than to not be in one.

*Did you always feel that way when you were in your other significant relationships?*

No, actually, I didn't. I felt restless part of the time and wanted to be alone. What an odd thing. What's wrong with me? When I was in a relationship, I craved being alone, and when I'm alone, I crave the closeness of a relationship. It's a feeling of knowing that you belong to someone. That's what I think it is…that I belong…that there is one person that cares about you more than anything.

*Oh, little one, is it that you want to belong…or that you "long to be?"*

Perhaps both. I also know that the wondering when, with whom, etc. steals from my peace. Not being in a relationship has brought up all kinds of stuff. It helped me to feel an ache in my heart over the summer.

*And you did some good writing through it, didn't you? Share with them the piece you wrote about the ache...you were right on target with that.*

## THE ACHE

There is an ache deep within me, one that I know well and one that knows me well. We've danced together for quite some time. When I allow myself to be with it, to simply feel it, it hurts, like a knife ripping the flesh around my heart.

It is the ache of longing, the ache of feeling like something is missing. It is the ache I feel when I see a couple embrace and feel the emptiness of space in my life...space that wants another body to share it.

It is the ache I feel when my clients tell their stories of losing a parent at a young age or of losing a child in an accident...or of losing love that was never "supposed" to end. As I hear their stories, I feel the wound in my heart begin to stir with a resonant familiarity...like tuning forks that vibrate together in the spirit of deep hurt. I know this ache won't kill me, but its depth pulls me in to the vast void of emptiness, leaving me wondering if I have the strength or the courage to feel it once again.

The tendency is to mask this ache...hoping for someone or something to divert my attention, so that I'll forget that it's there...even if only temporarily. As I sit with it, it brings me to an awareness that at its origin is the feeling of being separated from God...and the soul's longing to remember its connection.

But we mask it, we medicate it, sing about it, write about it, and I wonder...does everyone have this ache? If they were to truly sit in the silence of their thoughts, would they too feel it?

I notice something else. As I realize the energy it holds, the pain begins to subside...the tears slowly fade, and there is a gentle quiet where the pain was. What surprises me so often is how quickly and unexpectedly it can come on and how just as quickly and unexpectedly, it will dissipate.

My heart feels peaceful, and once again, I am reminded that there really is nothing ever to fear. But that the joy of being alive...of choosing to walk through this earth once again brings us to that dance again and again.

I offer thanks to all those who have brought me to that ache...despite my warnings to myself, and I am reminded that on some level, I may have asked them to carry me there. Thank you to all who had a part in it. For through this process, I realize that I am okay. My breaths continue...my heart still beats…I know I am home…in the peace of the stillness at the core of my being.

Perhaps it is the journey to the core of our being that is the most painful…for at the core of our being is the vast potentiality of God, and our journey there is not done through some mind exercises but an experience of sitting with what is in the heart. And the layers that have accumulated around the core are what holds the pain; it is the journey back to the heart that can hurt. The heart already holds peace, love, and joy… for we truly are the heart of God.

~~~~~~~~

*Yes, yes, yes, a resounding yes, but you are never separate from me—only in thought. I am with you always, but you cannot see or hear or feel me when you are in your pain…until you remember once again that I never left you.*

*If you only knew, little one, if you only knew how not alone you are in these thoughts. Not many are willing to feel it though. You are because you desire to see the truth through it. It is a dance…all of it, and you choreograph it all…inviting dance partners of all kinds to twirl and sway with you. There can be a joy in the dance; find your rhythm and know that all dance partners are there because you have asked for them.*

Thank you, God; I know that you care about us more than anything. And I don't mean to say that your love is not enough, but it's the physical kind of love that I'm talking about missing. I don't really mean sex, but about physical touch, cuddling…etc.

*But you have set in your mind that Divine Love is not enough. You may want to try it more often; Sandy, it will shift the ideas that you hold about being in a relationship. What are you afraid of?*

That if I tried it and devoted my heart to your love, then I wouldn't ever have the physical love. Maybe I'm afraid that I'd shut my heart out to physical love from another person because I wouldn't need it? I don't know. I'm a little confused about it.

*Sandy, it is quite the contrary; when you fill yourself with the Divine Love, you alter your physical being and would then attract a partner who would reflect that.*

So, how does one do that? I know I connect with you through this way and through prayer...but what do you mean exactly? I'm not sure I know how to do that; I have felt filled by your love many, many times. And I'm still in this same place—sometimes feeling an incredible amount of peace and sometimes feeling needy or empty.

*Do you start your day with that connection?*

No, not every day. But this past week when I've been writing with you, I feel like I've received a wonderful boost...especially when I write first thing in the morning.

*Good. You may want to start there. Before you get out of bed, bring love to the forefront of your mind and your presence. Breathe in love, breathe out love...imagine what that would feel like: becoming one with that energy of love...filling yourself with it. Vibrating with it...floating in the sea of it... being bathed in it and cleansed by it. Nothing else existing but love...that is being in the presence of God.*

It reminds me of what I recorded in the *Journey Home* meditation CD...releasing any fears, worries, anxieties, or concerns so that one can feel the presence of love that is always there.

*You've got it. You know how to do it, Sandy...do it more. It is exactly what I was referring to. The presence of love, my presence, is always there; it's just clouded over sometimes.*

Why don't we trust that that is enough? Why don't we spend more time being in that space?

*You already know the answer.*

I would think it's because we believe that more is better—bigger is better. In that *Jerry Seinfeld* DVD last night, he talked about how we've gotten accustomed to "Extra" Strength or "Maximum" Strength pain relievers...so much so, that "Strength" is not enough. In a way, we've gotten used to excess, and it hasn't filled the void; God, people still walk around emptier than ever because they now realize that what they thought would make them happy is not working long term. Are we really messed up here, or what?

*No. Watch the judgment. You're all awakening...some were sleepier than others. You are waking up to realize that no person, no place, no-thing can bring you peace or joy for the long term...because all people, places, and things change, die, and wear out, and if a person is attached to the object for peace or joy, then he or she will go from one object to the next, looking for the next "fix." You don't need "fixing"; you need loving. You need to feel my love, remember love, express love.*

Amen to that. And I do know that it is there for all...no matter how far one has strayed, right?

*Amen to that.*

*January 4*

Hey, God… So, what was up with the other night when I thought I had a robber in my house? Do people even call them "robbers" anymore? The kids were at Rich's house, Mikey and I were on the couch watching *Little Miss Sunshine*, and I swore I heard someone moving furniture upstairs! I heard it once, then dismissed it, heard it again…and got a little scared… then I heard it a third time and started to panic.

*What were your thoughts?*

First, I thought that there must be someone or something in the house….and all I had to protect me was a ten-pound, white furball, also known as Mikey, my Bichon Frise dog!

*What did you feel in your body?*

My hands started to shake; my heart raced, and I wanted to cry.

*So what did you do?*

I called Rich and whispered into the phone that I thought that someone was upstairs.

*Why didn't you call the police?*

Because I would have felt stupid if there was nothing there.

*And if there was?*

Why are you asking me that? I feel like I'm undergoing an investigation!

*Because on some level, if you really thought you were in danger, you would've called the police, right?*

Yes…but it didn't feel real enough.

*The fear didn't feel real enough. We'll get to that in a minute. So what happened?*

Within ten minutes, Rich came over with his wife's pit bull, Casie. They went through the whole house, every closet (ugh…stuff came falling out of my hall closet when he opened it), and every room, and nobody was hiding—not even behind the shower curtain.

*Did you feel better?*

Yes, because when Rich and Casie came over, I didn't feel like I was going through it alone.

*So what did you make of the whole thing?*

That it must have been someone in Spirit in the house (which still scares me!).

*Sandy, honey, you're a medium…you communicate with Spirit for your work…and you're scared that Spirit shows up at your house?*

I know it's silly, and I joke about it with my clients and groups that I teach. I've been asking to see Spirit for eleven years now to enhance the way I hear and feel them, but I imagine that actually seeing Spirit would scare me.

*We can look at that later, but what I want people to see from this "experience" of yours is this…*

I knew I'd be using my experiences to teach others. I'm taking one for the team?

*Yes, so let's look at what that night may have represented in the bigger picture. You heard something, a noise upstairs. Your thoughts about what it may have been—a robber or a non-physical being—brought fear to you. The fear was actually that you felt like you could have been harmed.*

Yes, and I knew as I was feeling it, that I couldn't get out of the fear mode...I was frozen in it.

*And your thoughts brought on a physical reaction—the shaky hands, racing heart—that then helped you to make a decision and take action—calling Rich. That led to another person responding—Rich coming over with the pit bull, which led to other thoughts that there was nothing physically there. And* **that** *led to peace. Is that right?*

Yes, but I'm not sure where you're going with this.

*You rarely are, and that is alright. You are a good student...willing to learn. Look at the process. An event triggered a thought, brought about a fear, brought on a physical reaction, caused a decision, created an action, spurred the response of others, which was followed by new thoughts and a new feeling.*

Okay...

*Many, Sandy, are going through the same process but are not aware of it. Let's look at a different scenario here. What are other ways this could've played out? Stay with me on this; it will all make sense. What are the different ways this could've played out?*

Hmm...if I heard the noise and if my kids or someone else was there with me, besides my little Bichon, I wouldn't have been scared.

*Good...why?*

Because I wouldn't have been by myself. I would've felt stronger with someone else there.

*Because you would've drawn strength from them?*

I guess, yes. For me, being alone triggers a fear that I am not strong in some ways...is that what you're getting at?

*But where are you learning to draw strength from when you are alone?*

From you.

*Bonus points for that answer, little one. And where do you think I was that night?*

I don't know...where were you?

*Right there with you. But you didn't ask…you didn't call out to me…you didn't try to draw strength from me. I'm not by any means putting any guilt or shame on you here. I want to show you that when you don't have an awareness of my presence, you feel the fear.*

You're absolutely right. The fear felt big to me, and I just reacted to it.

*As so many do, Sandy, as so many do. This is such a small example, but a good one to demonstrate what many people do when they let fear get big. They haven't called out my name and remembered that I am with them…always… in all ways. Remembrance of that will save many. You don't need saving for my sake; you need saving for your own peace of mind. To be "saved," is really to be "safe." You are already "safe"* **with** *me, which also means you are already "saved"* **with** *me. The only challenge for you in human form is that you forget that I am with you. Let me say that again…you forget that I am with you.*

*I am you…you are me…and we are one. How could we be separate? Jesus fully remembered my presence within him. That's why he was able to do what he was able to do…so too can you all.*

Wow…all that, from a few moments of thinking I had a robber or a ghost in my house?

*Sandy, it really wasn't about the noise at all…it was about helping you to see that you are always safe…with me. Whether your kids are there, or not, whether there is a man in your life or not.*

I get it…thank you. So, was there really a ghost here that night?

*Spirit is always with you Sandy, you know that. And yes, there was the presence of your maternal grandfather. But you were too afraid to ask who it may have been.*

You're right. I didn't want to know.

*He is with you often; he loves the writing that you do and draws close to your mom at this time to give her strength.*

She is going through a lot right now with my dad's lung cancer and her own bladder cancer. She could use his strength right now. Thank you…I will tell her…I know it's going to make her cry.

*It's okay; she needs the release. You will all be alright .*

I love you, God, thank you for always being there for us, even when we don't know that you are. Help us to remember.

*Always. I still want to address the comment of "the fear didn't feel real enough." That is such a common feeling. We'll do that next session.*

Thank you.

*January 8*

Good morning, God. Can we start where we left off last time? About us waiting for things to get too painful before we make changes?

*Good morning to you, little one. Yes, it is a common theme with many. People quite often will put off taking action, because the toothache is not painful enough; the job is not miserable enough; the abuse is not bad enough. So many wait until the pain grows so immense that it becomes unbearable, and they are unable to listen to what is in their hearts. Stop hurting yourselves like that. Take the time to listen to what your body tries to tell you about a situation; you will know...you will know...by your breath, by your "gut" feeling...by the heaviness or peace that you feel in your chest. Your body has such wisdom to it; take the time to listen. You will save yourselves much energy, which can then be used more creatively.*

Can everyone do that God? I mean, I too can sense when my body tells me that a situation is not right for me or when a decision or action isn't right—by the way my body reacts to the circumstances. But I don't always stand up for what my body instructs me to do. Oh my goodness, I have done that with food, knowing I'm full but still eating because it's yummy. I've done it with relationships, knowing that the relationship is not right for me but agreeing to be in it still. I've done it with work, overbooking my time with clients when I wanted to block out that time for me or for my kids. I've done it with myself physically, when my body was tired, but I pushed it to go food shopping (that could've easily waited until the next day). Shall I continue? I'm feeling a little vulnerable here…but I'm also seeing a pattern.

*And why do you think you do these things, when your body is telling you otherwise?*

Well, for the eating, I want to say because the food is so good…

*And you'll never get to eat it again?*

You're funny, God. I've joked that I must have starved to death in a previous lifetime because this thought inside me somewhere says, "Hoard food…there may not be enough later." I'm laughing because this thought presents itself in ways like making sure there is always more than enough chicken broth in the cabinet!

*Right, you must have been part of that chicken broth famine of 1842…*

Ha ha. It's a genetic thing. My sisters and I would always know when chicken broth was on sale at the grocery store because we'd find a case of College Inn chicken broth on our doorsteps, and we'd know our dad had been there delivering it to each of us! Shall I also mention that he and my mom have a few cases in their basement? But I digress here. Seriously, with the food thing, I sometimes don't pay attention to my body because I'd rather have the pleasure in the moment than think of the consequences later.

*Good insight. There are other reasons too. It fills something in the moment… not just your tummy.*

Yes, it fills a situation where I don't want to be bored, so I'll go looking for something to snack on. It also fills a circumstance when I need a distraction from writing or from cleaning or whatever else. It also serves me when I want a reward for doing something challenging.

*Good…what about relationships? How does not listening to your body's wisdom serve you or fill you?*

Hmm…it serves me in the way of not being alone…so I guess it fills a space of emptiness?

*Good…now what about work? How does overbooking yourself serve you when you know how much of a workload you can handle?*

For my work, overbooking ensures that there will be more than enough money to pay my monthly bills and indicates that I'm pleasing others. It can stem from my desire to help others; I think I like to feel needed. I'm hearing the Underdog song in my head, "Here I am to save the dayyyy...."

*And it is funny that when you went to type Underdog, you actually typed "Undergod" instead, which would be a healthier mindset for you to do your healing work in.*

Cute.

*Are there any other reasons that you can think of that may interfere with you not listening to your body?*

Hmmm...fear of hurting another's feelings, fear of not fitting in, fear of not having enough—they are all fear related. But I know I'm stronger than all this, and I don't live all of my life this way—just moments here and there.

*Sandy, you don't need to become defensive, little one. You are exposing parts of yourself here to help others see themselves in your words. I'm not judging you, so please don't go into judgment...that will only cause you to get stuck here. Remember that whatever you judge, you hold in your consciousness. So, look at these moments...learn from them, and try it differently next time. Believe you me, life will give you another opportunity to practice it again. So, in the spirit of learning, what happens when you don't operate from your body's wisdom but function from these fears instead?*

When I act from these fears, I feel like I've let myself down, which can lead to frustration and anger at myself. And, God, depending on the situation, I can become trapped in that spiral.

*What helps you come out of it?*

Usually remembering that I am connected to you...and that I am loved unconditionally no matter what...and forgiving myself for not choosing higher.

*Perfect. That is there for you always.*

God, but so many people here don't forgive themselves. I had a client once who asked me, "Sandy, is there anything that God won't forgive?"

44

*I know…I was there. Remember what you told her.*

I didn't mean to speak for you. I just shared what I know to be true in my heart of hearts.

*What you know to be true in your heart of hearts is all that I have revealed to you in your spirit before…so you spoke for me. Thank you for doing that. I want you to do it more.*

Thank you. I told her that there is nothing that God wouldn't forgive us for, but many things that we are unwilling to forgive ourselves for… and things that another human may not forgive us for. It made her think about her situation a little differently.

*Nice job—plant seeds…they grow when the individual is ready, which is sooner than you may think.*

And the client last night at the gathering I did God, who asked with desperation in her voice as she has struggled with alcoholism for years, "Sandy, do you think there is hope for me?" I told her, "Of course, because there is always God." Help me to help others, God.

*Let's look at the word "desperate." Look at it as "de-spirit" or as being away from spirit…from your spirit, from my spirit, which is the same essence. If you feel desperate, notice that you are not in tune with your own spirit, for when you are connected with spirit, you could never possibly feel desperate. When you are linked to the spirit, you are in-spirit or inspired. Look to these experiences of feeling desperate as times when you were out of alignment and notice what happened to your energy.*

How can we get back into alignment?

*Let me say this here to all that are reading these words…*
*The time is now…to let go of old hurts, old frustrations, old anger, and old habits. They block your full expression of joy here. There is always hope… no wound is too deep, no hurt too old, nothing that you could've done in the past is unforgivable, except by you. You are the only ones holding judgment on yourselves, and it continues to hurt you. Open your hearts and your minds to the potential of healing these things from your past. The shame, the guilt— you've all done it well…you've done it enough. It's time to stop hurting yourself with it. I am here for you for always…in all ways.*

*January 9*

God, I re-read what you just wrote about no wound being too deep and everything being forgivable. I'm reminded about a couple clients that I just worked with. One holds herself accountable for a young man's death twenty-five years ago; he jumped onto the hood of the bus she was driving, slipped under the wheel, and was killed. She was never charged for it—it wasn't her fault, but she has lived for the last twenty-five years thinking that you are going to punish her for it, so she doesn't dare get too happy. Her mom died six months ago, and her sister just committed suicide two weeks ago. She thinks it's part of your punishment for her.

*I know. I was there with you in the session...you asked me to be. You did the right thing by having her imagine that she was having a face-to-face conversation with me.*

I brought her back to the memory twenty-five years ago, back to the young woman that she was. That younger version of her held onto so much guilt and fear of retribution. So, yes, I did have her bring you into it.

*It was perfect.*

And I asked her to ask you directly, "God, are you trying to punish me?"

*And do you remember what I said directly to her? I told her, "No, I am not trying to punish you, but you have been trying to punish yourself all these years; it's time to stop."*

46

Yes, it made me want to cry. I so hoped you would say that, and I knew it would more greatly affect her if she imagined standing in front of you directly and heard it right from your essence…rather than me telling her what I believe to be true.

*It's a sign of a good teacher, Sandy.*

Thank you…I really knew what you'd say to her, and you didn't let me down nor do you ever, now that I think about it. You helped my client yesterday too. She so feared not being able to help her siblings the way she thought she should because they're in such chaos right now. She was afraid that she is failing them. So I had her bring you into her mind, and ask you directly, "God, am I failing?"

*And remember what I said to her…*

Yes, you said, "No, you are not failing; it is not your job to save them." It brought her a lot of relief. God, why don't we think to go to you first? It seems almost too simple…to go to you directly with our fears: Am I failing? Am I enough? Am I where I am meant to be? But instead of asking you directly, we ask everyone around us, but it doesn't seem to help.

*Many don't even **ask** the question—AM I failing? AM I enough? They assume that they are. Most ask…WHY do I keep feeling like I'm failing? WHY do I not feel like I'm enough? WHY am I confused as to my path? The question WHY keeps many stuck or digging for an answer that may never satisfy them.*

So, how can we ask it differently then? Many people are intent on knowing why. I hear it from my clients all the time: "Why did he die now? We were just enjoying the best days of our relationship…" "Why did he die before I got there? I was in the car on the way to the hospital." Why? WHY?

I understand the soul's answers to these questions. The soul would say it was the way it was: everything happens for a reason. But that doesn't do much for the person in pain. They want to know WHY.

*The "whys" are not wise. They get you nowhere, but they bring you now-here, which is a good idea for anyone who is in pain. And being now-here will help you to come into the moment to help you to recognize what's truly underneath the insistent question of **WHY**: **What's Hurting You?** When one* *doesn't want to truly look at the hurt, they'll ask why. When one doesn't want to be now-here with their pain, they'll feel nowhere…lost. When one has reached the point of having enough pain, they will allow the healing of the hurt, which leads to healing of the heart.*

How, God? How can they do that?

*It is simple. Love and forgiveness. It is that simple. You can go through it in one of two ways: the sleepy path or the awakened path. You choose it on some level.*

We do?

*Yes, think of it this way. On the sleepy path, one feels pain; one asks why and goes into blame and victimization, which brings them into continual hurt, pain, blame. They keep asking why and keep the energy alive by continuing to tell the story around it. Finally at some point, they may realize that the energy gets them nowhere. They may awaken to the specific thoughts that truly hurt them. If they ask to see the situation differently, they realize that the life experience offers growth, learning, and healing, and they may then see the gift that the situation held for them. That's where love, forgiveness, and strength are remembered.*

*On the awakened path, in a very simplified explanation, one has now-here awareness already. One understands that a gift or lesson exists in the situation and asks for it to be revealed. Peace follows shortly. Remember, there is no judgment other than the judgment you place on yourself for either path that you choose.*

*January 11*

1/11—Angel Day…"111"; it's also my sister Cindy's birthday…happy birthday, Cindy…I need to call her to wish her a happy birthday.

God, my heart has been pondering the many people around me being bombarded with such tough challenges. One of my girlfriends had a beautiful twenty-year marriage and her husband just told her that he realizes he is gay. Another friend told me that her cousin just died and she had three young children. Yet another friend shared that he feels like he's been in a coma for the past seven years and is now waking up, but he's scared and alone and worries he is experiencing a breakdown. My mom, who is so wonderful and loving, faces exhaustion as she tries to be strong for my dad with all of his health challenges. And lately so many clients have said, "I just don't want to be here anymore. It's too hard." I feel like we need extra help here. I feel like I'm supposed to connect with you to be filled, so that I can continue to be strong for everyone else. But sometimes, the burden of everyone else's pain is too much for me to handle.

*It is too much for you to handle…alone. But I am here for you. You may think you're going to crack your exterior strength, but that is okay; I am here for you always. For your friend who feels like he is going to have a breakdown, that is okay as well. So many of you try to be so strong to keep the fight going. What are you all fighting against?*

I think we're fighting against falling apart or feeling weakened.

*What do you imagine would happen if you fell apart or felt weakened?*

Then we'd be in little pieces and unsure which shards fit and which slivers don't.

*And if one felt weakened?*

Then I guess some would be afraid that they'd be tempted to indulge in past behaviors again; some would turn to alcohol, some would turn to depression, and some would lash out in anger, I guess.

*Dearest little one, let's look at the words: turn to…lash out…*

Okay, but once again, I'm not sure where you're going.

*The words reflect an external reaching out. Look at what they "turn to"—all things that have held fear, pain, and hurt. They can just as easily choose to turn in to love…to turn to God.*

I don't know how easy it is for them, God, because these things have had such a hold on them.

*Do they? Or do these **individuals** have a hold on the alcohol, on the depression, etc.? If they were to look at it truly, they would see that they cling to it out of fear that without it they would sink and have no identity. It is a habitual response, which has given them a familiar feeling. See if that is true with your friend who fears a breakdown. Understand what it is for him.*

*Alcohol is not the disease; the thoughts within the mind of the alcoholic are dis-eased. Depression is not a disease; the thoughts within the mind of the individual who is depressed are dis-eased. All these things you mention can be traced to thoughts within the mind that are dis-eased—not in alignment with love, with God. All are a call for healing at the thought level. Look at the thoughts; bring them to a new vibration…the vibration of love.*

The idea that one is weak is not a bad thing? To fall apart is not a bad thing?

*No, stop fighting it: Let yourself feel "weak" or fall apart if you need to because ultimately, you will reach the end point—the point of no return—which is alright, because I am there. Wherever you go, there I am.*

*There is already a love within each of you that was placed there at birth… an energetic imprint of love. Each of you came here on a journey to remember that love. Some of you are lost because you thought love was something to be found or generated outside of you, something you tried to "bring in" and "keep it as yours."*

*However, what many of you are discovering is that what you have felt attached to as a source of love or of comfort (whether it be a positive influence as in a relationship or a negative influence, such as alcohol) is shifting, and it scares the hell out of you. That is good—better to get the hell out of you than to keep it in you! All these moves can bring you to a remembrance of the divine imprint of love within you...to the remembrance of my love. It is there for all. When you remember it, life is never the same for you again. These shifts are not easy ones. They are like labor pains...like contractions...that can hurt. All lead to potential new birth...re-birth...giving birth to what has already been within you—an awakened heart that remembers love.*

So when people feel like they're "coming undone" or that they're having a "breakdown," it's not all bad, is it?

*Sandy, not only is it not bad, it is a sign that a breakthrough is present for them. The term "coming undone" is often used when people have wrapped themselves in an illusion that they've bought into. There is much that I'd like to share about illusions. There is not much that is real and lasting on earth, but yet you hold on to earthly things like your life depends on it—onto other people, your jobs, your possessions, your ideas about who you think you are. You hold on to it all for dear life and place your trust there, believing that those external things will always be there for you the way you need them to be.*

*This I can guarantee you: They may not, not in the way that you may need them to be. And here is where you get yourself wrapped up in expectations, and then when those expectations are not met, trust is destroyed, and you feel alone and hurt. Right?*

Yes, you're absolutely right.

*Know, dearest ones, that part of your learning in human form is to know and understand what it is that you can trust. It is on your currency: "In God We Trust." But do you really? If you would, there would be far less hurt, anger, and illness.*

But, God, many clients have shared with me that they have trusted you, have been "let down," and have not trusted after that. I don't mean to sound negative, but that is what I hear from so many.

*Yes, they have been let down, but it is because they have trusted in me only to provide a particular outcome, yes?*

Yes, I hear from clients, "I'm trusting God to take care of this money problem. I'm trusting that God will make my loved one better." And when it doesn't turn out how they prayed for, they're upset.

Oh, God, I'm reminded of when Talia was in the hospital, when my life changed. I prayed at the beginning, "God you *have* to make Talia better," because that was the only way I envisioned that I'd be able to survive . But it was torture every day because one day she'd be okay, then the next she'd have to go back on the ventilator for life support because she wasn't breathing well on her own. It was like a roller coaster ride—a scary one.

*And how did your life shift?*

My life changed when I began praying, "God, give me the strength to get through whatever I need to here." It was then that I started having more peace even in the midst of the chaos. I began to realize that no matter what, I'd be okay.

*How did you know that?*

Somehow, I knew you were with me. I want to cry right now, thinking of all those that don't feel that you are with them. I want them to know. And I want them to know that this is not a religious thing but a spiritual experience.

*That is why we are doing this book, Sandy. They will know I am here for them…through all the experiences you'll be revealing from your life. You'll help them to see that no matter whether it is in the larger experiences or in the mundane parts of life, I am there.*

Why do I feel like crying? It is so darn simple, God. Why have we forgotten?

*Little one, cry if you need to. You are remembering the power of love. Bring it to others. I'll show you the way. Stay focused on the task at hand, which is this writing.*

I love you, God.

*I love you too, all of you...each and every one of you who is reading this book...and even those who aren't. My love for you is the same. However, you need to feel it—paternal, maternal, fraternal love—the one commonality... it is eternal.*

*So, yes, you may have been let down when you've trusted me and a certain event didn't go your way, and you have a little tantrum. It doesn't stop me from loving you still. But think of this...have I ever let anyone down when it came to feeling my love? MY love, not love from another human being. There's a big difference. Love from a human being is really a reflection of how open one is to my love anyway. So yes, there may be many disappointments in your life, but my love never disappoints...it is there for all.*

*The same is true for forgiveness. There is no need for forgiveness from me because I already love you unconditionally—and that holds an understanding that you grow through all of your experiences. Each of you plays out the dramas of your choice, and you'll continue to play out the drama until you tire of it. Then you'll understand what conscious creation is about.*

*January 12*

Hey, God, I spoke to my mom today. She's read the first forty pages of this manuscript, and guess what she said?

*That she loved it?*

Yes, and that it reminds her to pray to you. How cool is that? I have to tell you though that all this God and prayer talk—in the earlier part of my life—would have turned me off.

*Why?*

Because it felt so…not real…not personal to me. It seemed like someone always wanted me to pray a certain way, believe in a certain way, and then I was suppose to feel a certain way, but I have to tell you, it never worked for me. Not in the manner that they told me, but definitely in the method that I have come to know you in these last twelve years since Talia's birth and death. That was when you became real to me, even though we didn't really directly converse. The God I knew and loved helped me go on with life after Talia—not the God associated with fear, repentance, hell, and damnation. That God just didn't feel real to me.

*It's not who I am to you.*

I know that now. And prayer, God, I couldn't pray like people told me to. "Oh Lord, grant us that…." That didn't feel right to me either. So, I used to think, "I'm not doing this right. I'm not connecting to the 'right' God."

*There is more than one of me?*

LOL. No. You are the essence of love of all that is, but here we sure see you differently.

*And some even create wars over it. But let's not go there right now. Go back to your idea of not feeling like you weren't praying "right."*

Well, for me, saying the Lord's Prayer involved just repeating words. Trying to read the Bible with the thee's, thou's, and shalt's, I could never make sense of any of it. I knew in my heart that that is not how you would talk to us now. When I went to Medjugorje six years ago and learned to pray the rosary, I didn't connect with the essence of what I said. I was reciting words, and the words didn't do anything for me.

*Do you know how many are going to relate to what you are admitting to?*

Not really…but thank you.

*You don't have to pray in a certain way for me. I understand the way you speak. You don't talk to each other using thee's, thou's, and shalts nor do you need to talk to me that way. Your prayer doesn't have to be "formal" just give it a "form." Give your thoughts form, and that becomes your prayer.*

I like that.

*And you know that when you pray, you are doing that for you.*

What?

*When you pray from your heart, you feel my energy, the piece of me, the "peace" of me within your heart. And when you hear my response, it would be a good idea that you not only hear my words but become my words. You just suggested that to your client yesterday—nice job.*

Thanks, I don't know where that came from.

*Hello…*

I know, I know, from me/you/one. But to become God's words, what does that really mean?

*Sandy, some people hear my words; yet some still choose not to integrate them in their hearts. Some people know them in their spirits; yet some still choose not to act on what they know…to fully integrate what they know. They are not "becoming God's words." No judgment, just for you to notice. So, many of my words remain as an idea, a thought that sounds good to them.*

Is it because they can't or won't or don't know how or maybe are afraid to fully integrate your words?

*Some fear their creative power. When you "integrate," you will move "intogreat"-ness. But when you aren't connecting with the essence of what you are praying, it doesn't do anything for you. It is similar to individuals not linking to the essence of who I am and feeling like I'm not doing anything for them.*

Yes.

*And what they do is give up. Many pray to me, but not all listen for my response. They may not think it is possible. They may not want to stop the distractions that interfere with them perceiving my response. It's hard for people to hear my thoughts through their iPod earpieces!*

I know, and I did give up on praying…for a while. But this is different, God; you're funny…you're like a real friend to talk to—who will answer me in ways that I can understand. You speak my language!

*Would you rather I spoke German to you?*

See what I mean? You're hilarious, and I can so relate to your humor! Going to the Armenian church as a kid—where half the service was in English and half was in Armenian—oh, God, I didn't have a clue. We kids didn't understand Armenian (except for foods and body parts!). My sisters and I would end up passing notes back and forth to each other, and one of us would start to laugh; then before you know it, we'd be laughing uncontrollably, almost to the point of snorting, and then the more we'd try to stop, the worse it would get!

*I know, I was there.*

Were you angry with us for not paying attention?

*Sandy, I didn't need you to pay attention for my sake. The experience was for what you needed to get out of it. No, I wasn't angry, but your mom didn't like it too much!*

I know. And I've been there with my own kids, wanting them to "get" something from church so badly, but it wasn't at their level.

*Your kids know about me.*

I don't take them to church though.

*They know about me.*

But I don't always talk about you to them.

*They know about me because you show them love. Continue to teach them about love...teach them how to surrender to love. Let them know I am with them always.*

God, I will admit something else too. Starting out with "Our father, who art in heaven...," there are times when I needed you to be like a big strong father figure to me, and you were. But this part of "who art in heaven" makes you seem so far away. To many people, in fact, heaven feels so distant. That's why we wanted to create a kids' book to help kids who have lost a parent.

*I know, who do you think inspired your friend's ideas for it on her ride home from your office?*

You. You really are always there...in essence...for all. I think as I was growing up, my idea of you, God, was that you were like a cosmic Santa Claus. If I was good enough, then maybe, just maybe, you'd make me skinny; or in junior high school, you'd "make" the boy I had a crush on like me back.

*Sandy, that's the idea that many of you hold about me—that I "make" things happen. Here's where you'll be helping so many here. I don't "make" things happen.*

Oh, God, here go the gasps from the readers...

*I don't.*

Who does?

*You do…you all do with your energy. You attract it all into your life. Yes, there is a blueprint for life, but the details are where your own free will comes in.*

When I read what you just wrote, I wanted to shout out "Free Will-y"! I didn't see the movie, but I'm wondering if there's a message in it for us.

*You may want to rent it then; that will be your homework. But let's get back to the idea we were on before your beautiful creative mind took off. When you align your energy to love, miracles happen. Look at the word* miracle. *Its root is "mira"…to see. Miracle…to "see" differently.*

Can we go slower with this concept?

*Sure, I've got nothing but time. In the old mindset, a miracle was "cast down by God" to those who were "favored." Let me share something with you: I don't play favorites.*

So, why are some people healed and then claim it is a miracle from you? Are you not the one doing the healing?

*I am always the energy of healing, but I am not the one DOING the healing. You all are…or not. But there is no judgment on who does not get "healed," for many of you feel that physical healing is the only way to peace. Sometimes the body has carried the spirit for its job, and the spirit can now move to another dimension, so the healing is done at another level, and the individual can transition out of the body. So many of you there, though, think that you've failed, that you haven't prayed hard enough, that you couldn't heal a loved one. If the soul was destined to be healed, it would have been. Let go of the judgment and the idea of failing to heal.*

God, with my client yesterday, I don't know if I helped her or not. She has struggled all her life with unworthiness, so I encouraged her to visualize standing before you and asking, "Am I worthy?" But she couldn't feel you around her at all. She said, "I guess God turned his back on me."

*Why would I do that?*

That's what I asked her. She said, "Because of all the terrible things I've done in my life." I told her that she could borrow my concept of a loving God who is there for us always no matter what—that you would never turn your back on us because you are love, and love simply loves. But she couldn't buy into that.

*And so you felt like you failed her because she chose to not hold on to a loving thought? Isn't that what we were just writing about yesterday?*

Yes, I did feel that, but only for a little while. I could somehow see that she wasn't accepting a loving thought about you. She wouldn't allow herself to forgive herself…and that was what kept her in her pain.

*You actually used the words, "if you hold onto this idea, you will continue to be in your hell," didn't you?*

Yes, I did.

*It is truth. Many keep themselves in their own version of hell, but they don't need to be there. "Heaven" is experiencing the **reflection of love**. "Hell" is experiencing the **rejection of love**. Both are your choices. Your client felt what it is like to reject love.*

But she doesn't know what love is; she never experienced it even as a kid.

*And through hypnosis, you regressed her back to when she was a child and helped her inner child to accept love…to remember my love, right?*

Yes, and the inner child received it and felt free, but the adult part of her couldn't move past the idea that you turned your back on her. God, you are blamed for many things, you know.

*I know, it's okay; when people need someone or something to blame, it is merely a reflection of a lack of love. I am still there with them always.*

Another client I had yesterday, she said that she is furious with you because her son died two years ago in a sudden car accident, and she thinks you "took" him. I went out on a limb to stick up for you.

*Sandy, you don't need to protect me, but what you did was speak truth to her illusion.*

Thank you. I told her, "God didn't 'take' your son. It was his time to die, according to his soul contract." I helped her to process her pain. Where do we get that idea from anyway? Some people think that you "take" people and that's why they die or that you "needed" them, so you "took" them. That never made sense to me.

*Because it is not true. So many do not understand death from the soul's perspective. You had a chance to share truth. Thank you.*

No, thank you, for having given me the wisdom of your truth.

*It is there for all.*

*January 15*

God, as I'm in this dialog with you, it's interesting to hear how others think about you. When I spoke to a friend yesterday, he kept saying that we had to fear you, that in order to respect you, we had to fear you. I don't see it that way at all; I don't fear you; I don't imagine you have wrath or vengeance. I love you and want to draw closer to you.

*You cannot get any closer because I am within you; your heart beats with my energy. So, let's look at where your friend came up with this idea that he had to fear me.*

Well, he mentioned that his dad used to beat him when he was a kid. I'm sensing that had a big part in his idea of you?

*It does for many. Their relationships with their parents often dictate their ideas about me...for a long while...until they are willing to look at it differently. So his relationship with his father was strained right?*

That's an understatement.

*So for him, he may equate "love" with "fear" because if he expected love from his dad but received physical pain and fear, then his distorted idea of love was molded at an early age. It is not truth, but it became his truth. So in his relationships, did he also use fear to connect with others?*

Yes, I think he did; he has an edge that I think he uses to protect himself. He's always ready for a fight.

*And his father "made" him obey out of fear, right?*

Yes, and it sort of translates into how he sees you to be.

*That is not how I operate. I am love. I don't "make" anybody do anything. You all choose out of your highest ideas about who you are. As you grow and evolve, you begin to see yourselves more lovingly, and then your actions reflect more love. It is all about recalling who you are in love. His father didn't have a loving understanding about me either.*

It brings me back to my client who thought you had turned your back on her. Wow, this works with her too. She told me that she always thought her dad hated her, and that he had never been there for her. And so it may have translated into her ideas of who she thinks you are? Wow, wow, wow.

*Yes, sad to say, yes. Hopefully, this book will help others to see who I am and who they are as well. We are one. But let's get back to this idea of fear vs. respect.*

Okay.

*To earn respect has nothing to do with operating from a place of fear. Yes, you may earn respect from someone, but the roots will not be deep. Respect is a choice as is any other action. When you teach from fear, you instill fear. When you "instill fear," you are "in fear still." Not a judgment, but something to look at. When you teach from love, you help people to see themselves from that loving place as well; you become a reminder that they are loveable…worthy of love.*

I like that. It makes so much sense.

*So, when you want to earn respect from someone, be it a child or an employee, demonstrate how you treat yourself with respect, which will help you to treat them with respect. They will then have a better chance of modeling that behavior for themselves.*

You are the coolest! Thank you.

*You are more than welcome, Sandy. You are all welcome anytime.*

*January 18*

Good morning, God. My dad returned to the hospital today because he was having a hard time breathing this morning. They don't think it's from his lung cancer but from his heart issues. I planned to visit my parents this morning, but my mom will be at the hospital with my sister Cindy...and they told me not to go. So, here I am—confused and a little conflicted. I'm not sure what to feel. Part of me feels like I should be "doing" something, going somewhere to be useful, and part of me wonders why I'm not worried, and I'm feeling a little guilty about it.

*What are you feeling guilty about?*

That I'm not worried. But I do feel like there's a well of sadness that is there; I'm just not tapping into it right now.

*So can you let it be? It will be accessible to you when you feel you need it to be.*

Okay. Any insight on my dad that we need to know?

*His body is going through many changes. It has served him well for eighty-two years. A part of you wants to fill in the blanks right now. You have an "unknown" space...not knowing what is going to happen next, not knowing what his body will do or how long he will be here...*

Yes, that's very true, and I know my mind will try to fill in the blanks, usually with stuff that I imagine holds fear.

*Do you know why you do that?*

Ummm…to prepare myself…to imagine the worst, so that I can brace myself for it to prepare for it.

*And what do you do to "prepare"?*

Good questions today…not sure I have the answers though.

*You really do…within. You all do. When you remember them, you would know you wouldn't need to prepare for anything, but only be willing to show up in the moment…fully present.*

Ok, so what do I do to prepare? I start picturing the worst possible scenario and start to process the sadness, so it doesn't take me by surprise because at least I know that when I take myself to the middle of sadness I can embrace it. But if it takes me by surprise, I tend to brace against it. Does that even make sense? I don't know if it does to me or if that even answers your question. Actually, I'm so distracted that I don't even know what your question was, God, so sorry.

*It's alright little one. Actually, you are right there with an important piece of wisdom. Let's look at it.*

I love when you say, "Let's look at it." I feel like I'm being loved into the lesson.

*You are, so let's look at it. When you take yourself into sadness, you feel that you are able to embrace it. But when life takes you there by surprise, you often feel you need to brace yourself against it. Is there a fear there?*

I'm not sure if it's fear, but hmmm….let me think a minute. Why am I drawing a blank here? Can you help me to see it?

*Sandy, for many of you, your need to be in control often dictates how you show up in the moment. You are describing a feeling of being out of control. When you are taken by surprise, it is really a feeling of not being in control. So, let's go there because it affects so many of you.*

*When you are not in control, you imagine that someone or something outside of you can harm you. Sit with that for a minute. You'll see that it's true for you. It stems from old beliefs. That someone or something will come and hurt you. Whether you are ready for it or not, life sometimes hurts, and you know in your heart that when you brace yourself for something, you physically* set up a situation in your body…a rigidness that can actually cause more harm than help. You just saw it on the news this morning.

Yes, I did. A bull was trampling a bullfighter, and the clowns tried to distract the bull, but it kept stepping on the bullfighter. The reporter said the bullfighter wasn't injured because he went unconscious, and so his body relaxed. Is that what you mean? But surely you're not telling us to be unconscious through life. I know that's not what you mean.

*Exactly the opposite. I wish for you all to wake up…in full consciousness to the fact that nothing and no one outside yourself can hurt or harm you. And when you realize that, you will recognize there is nothing to brace against… nothing to be prepared for.*

Oh, God, how can that be…I'm struggling a little bit with this. How can you say that nothing and no one outside ourselves can cause hurt or harm?

*Sandy, let me break it down. There are three parts to what I just gave you. Let's take this slowly. First, you are all one…there is nothing outside of yourself. You see yourselves as separate, and that is your experience. You hold the idea of enemies, and it becomes part of your reality. You hold the idea first, and then it becomes your reality. It's the law of the universe.*

*Second, nothing causes any emotion. Emotion—e-motion or "energy" in motion—is already within you. The energetic wounds of hurt, sadness, anger, etc. are already within each of you. When an event happens in your life, something is triggered within you. It is not a bad thing but more an opportunity for you to see what energy you hold within yourself. The same event can trigger a variety of emotions in different people. What evokes anger in one may evoke compassion or sadness in another. It is already there within you.*

*Third, the idea of hurt and harm…please look at how you judge those… and keep yourselves stuck in their energy. Look to see the ideas you hold around being "hurt" or "harmed." What have you decided it means about who others are, who you are, and how you define your life? When you have a cut, your body possesses a natural ability to heal itself, right? You don't have to watch over it, telling the body, "Heal! Heal!" Your body knows what to do. You would be surprised at the body's ability to heal itself if you would only watch the fearful thoughts you cling to when you are in a time of sickness.*

This was a lot you just gave me, but I feel we got off track. (Oh, God, listen to me. I'm telling God that he got off track!)

65

*It's all connected; let's go back. We were talking about you needing to be in control. When you feel that you aren't in control, you fear what may happen. It all goes back to the truth that nothing can harm you…not even death.*

I think I understand that because death is not the end.

*Amen. Death is the end of the physical existence of the functioning body but not the end of you.*

Because who we are is not our body.

*Yes, and do you know who you are?*

I know the answer you're looking for: We are you; we hold your energy in physical form. That's the ultimate of who we are, and that cannot be hurt or harmed or destroyed.

*Yes.*

Then why do so many here struggle so much? Emotionally, physically, God, all you have to do is turn on the TV to see the drug commercials, the lawyers trying to "fix" the pain, trying to alleviate what's "hurting" people.

*Because people identify with what they think hurts them; they feel that something is injuring their pride, their pocketbook, their ego, their body, their sense of who they think they are. Maybe it's time for people to look at what's really "hurting" them.*

And that would be…

*Not feeling loved in all the places they've kept hidden from view.*

That feels so peaceful. And sounds so simple. Can we go back to this idea of not being in control?

*Sure, it is tied to a feeling of needing to protect something people think they will lose.*

Wow, this is pretty deep.

*It can be, but it is so simple. What do you imagine people are afraid of losing? Let's go one by one, alright?*

Okay. I know that people are afraid of losing their loved ones.

*And what do you know about that?*

You're asking lots of questions today. Well, I know that we can't really "lose" anyone because when someone dies, they simply change form. They exist as Spirit. What we miss though is the physical form that we were used to.

*Exactly. What else do you imagine there is fear around losing?*

Honest to God, I feel like I'm playing Family Feud: "Here are the top answers to the question, 'What people are afraid of losing?' Survey says…" Okay, sorry. People are also frightened by the thought of losing their money.

*Yes, they are deathly afraid of losing their money. And what do you know about that?*

Well, I know that money is just paper and metal. But our idea about money is energetically charged in one way or another. The energy idea of money flows like a current. Maybe that's why they call it currency? Sometimes it flows to us, and sometimes it flows from us. I've had it, I've lost it, and it has always returned. I know that you really can't lose it, but it changes hands.

Three years ago, I experienced a big financial loss. I'd invested in a bed and breakfast in Plymouth, MA and lost everything I'd put into it (which was nearly all the money I'd received from my divorce). That hurt and was very scary for me. I'll never forget the morning I sat at my kitchen table in my little condo, thinking, "Oh, God, how does one get through this? How do you start over again after a loss this big?"

*And do you remember what I said to you then?*

I'll always remember it. You said, "Sandy, I got you through the 'loss' of your daughter. Do you not think I will help you get through this too?" That changed everything for me. I felt such peace, and it helped me to let go of the worry, which enabled me to turn things around, and I've bounced back nicely.

*Good. Because I will always help you to remember that no matter what, you will always be okay. There is always an opportunity to return to peace and feel loved and allow life to flow through you again.*

I've noticed that when we hold negative energy—fear, worry, anxiety, guilt—around financial loss, we won't be able to see the other side of it as easily...to be in a position to attract abundance as easily.

Oh my God, the same thing occurs when someone loses a loved one. Loved ones in Spirit have said to me that when we hold onto worry, anxiety, and guilt around the loss, we won't feel their presence around us. They try to send their thoughts to us and put their energy around us, but it's like we're surrounded by a bubble of negativity and they can't penetrate that. Wow...there really are some similarities here.

*Yes, let's keep going. What else are people afraid of losing?*

Hmm...people fear losing their outer beauty, their vitality, and their youth.

*So what do they do?*

Some become obsessed about keeping it. With surgeries, pills, creams, diets, and exercises, it's a multi-billion dollar industry fueled by what we see on TV...ugh.

*Is it real?*

No, it's not. Not to me. I know that a person's age is in their mindset.

*Yes, and in truth...or love, there is no time.*

Is that why when people "fall in love," many say that they feel young again?

*Yes, partly. But there is an eternal, ageless beauty.*

How?

*It involves releasing the expectation that you need to look a certain way to be loved and to love. You know people who are beautiful on the outside, but hold something so different on the inside that no outer beauty could make up for it.*

Yes.

*It all goes back to where one is willing to put their energy and attention. Inner beauty, inner peacefulness, inner calm helps the outer more than you realize. It brings a different energy to every cell within you—one that is loving.*

*And love is the greatest healer of all. What else can you think of that people are afraid of losing?*

Their status in life? Their hair maybe? Their reputation… their business…their spouse to another person?

*Sandy, there is a similar thread to all of these things. All "loss" is an external idea. Internally, there can be no loss because you are not separate from me. I will say this to the end of all time. There can be no loss because you are not separate from me. Whatever you think you are losing…let it go. If it is meant to be in your life, it will return, perhaps not in the same form, but changed in some way. This is where letting go of control comes back in full circle. When you fear "loss," you tend to try to be in control. But there is no "loss" so you can release the need to control…and allow life to flow.*

Okay, I have to go pee. Oh, God, I can't believe I just told you I have to go pee. I'll be right back.

~~~~~~

I'm back.

*I'm still here.*

So, can you help us to know how to let go of control? It sounds like such an easy concept.

*Teach them how you do it.*

Well, I do a few things. First, I identify what it is that I'm trying so hard to control. Usually for me, it's about being attached to a certain outcome that I think will make me happy. And fear can enter…"WHAT IF IT DOESN"T HAPPEN?" Or if I'm faced with an unknown, again fear can come in and force me to believe that I have to work hard and do whatever I can to ensure the scary outcome doesn't occur. It hardly ever works, so then I surrender it to you.

*How?*

I picture in my mind's eye giving the situation, the person, the concern, etc. to you. I have come to know that there is always a divine solution. It just may be out of my sight in the moment if I'm focused on fear or worry.

*And what do you feel afterwards?*

Peace…so much peace because I know I'm not in this alone. But the funny thing is that I may have to surrender something over and over again because I find that after I've "given" it to you, I sometimes take it back, and my mind starts trying to figure it out or fix it again.

*So sweetly human. You all do that…until you don't anymore.*

Yes. And I've also found that surrendering helps me to stay open to divine guidance and intuition that will lead me exactly where I need to be because I can't always see my way clearly when I'm befuddled with anxiety. Oh, wow, I don't think I've ever used that word before…befuddled. It's a cute word and reminds me of Elmer Fudd. Befuddled….befuddled… befuddled.

*And when you are done being "befuddled," you will "be fueled" by my presence and love.*

I love it! I love when you play on words like that. It's fun to me.

*Glad to be of service, Sandy. You're easy to amuse. Fun is a good thing; it feels better to you than drama, doesn't it?*

Yes!

*Not a judgment, just noticing that you all have dramas that play out in life. How hooked into them are you? How have you let the dramas define you or rather…"deafen" you to my voice?*

Ooh, good one, God!

*You decide what the drama means to you or about you. There is a feeling associated with it. You choose, consciously or unconsciously, the vibration of thoughts you hold. So I say to you, "choose higher." I mean that there is always another way you can choose to think about a situation you're experiencing—a way that holds not fear but love and hope. You all have decided what you imagine is true for you. I'm suggesting that there is a higher truth, one aligned with peace and love.*

Can I give them a real life example?

*Please do.*

Alright, here's one that I worked with about a month before I started writing this book. I experienced some anxiety that I wanted to be writing more and speaking to larger audiences. You told me to look at the thoughts around it and the vibration of the feelings associated with those thoughts. So, here is what I had written.

**My situation: I should be reaching more people.**

| Thoughts I can hold around this situation: | Vibration of the thoughts: |
|---|---|
| I should already be there! | Shame, guilt |
| Others are so far ahead of me. | Shame, fear |
| I'm stuck. | Fear |
| What if it doesn't ever happen? What if I can't focus? What if I don't know where to start? | Fear |
| What message do I even want to share? All my experiences in the last couple years have given me the wisdom to help others. | Hope |
| My audience is waiting. People have loved my writings and workshops in the past. | Joy |
| I love creating and writing. | Joy |
| I am in the right place at the right time. | Peace |
| It's not really about me. "God, inspire me through my written and spoken word. Show me the way." | Peace |

You helped me to see that I can look at the "drama" in many different ways.

*Yes, and whichever thought you're holding in your mind...let it be okay. Be conscious of it. As you make the connections between the thoughts and the vibrations of those thoughts, you can ask yourself, "What DO I want to feel?" If you want to feel happy or peaceful, you will need to shift your thoughts to a higher vibration. You cannot cling to a thought that holds the vibration of guilt and shame and be peaceful at the same time.*

I know. I have tried this and tested it out in so many areas of my life, and it works every time. I take the thought that holds the highest vibration (peace or love) and cling to that thought. I think about it, maybe write it down, and keep it somewhere that I will be reminded of it, and I feel peace.

*Remember this, all who are reading these words, it is not the situation that causes the feeling, but it is the thought that you hold about it. Sandy, give them another example. I know it's personal, but give them the one about not being in a relationship right now. Many will be able to relate.*

Ugh...ok, but it makes me feel vulnerable. Another situation I worked out with this process was not presently being in a relationship. Throughout the last few months, I alternated between being truly peaceful with it and feeling sad about it, so...

**My situation: I'm not currently in a relationship.**

| Thoughts I can hold around it: | Vibration of the thoughts: |
|---|---|
| Feeling left out...seems like everyone has someone special except me. | Sad, lonely |
| It's easier for everyone else to find someone. | Sad |
| Maybe there's something wrong with me. | Sad |
| Maybe I'm doing this dating thing wrong. | Scared |
| I'm unlovable. | Sad |
| This has given me time to heal old emotional wounds. | Peace |
| I actually like my alone time. | Peace |
| This has given me time to become really clear about who I am and what I really would like in a relationship. | Peace |
| I have completed karmic ties to my former husband and former relationships since my divorce. I am free. | Peace |
| This time has brought some wonderful writing pieces forth and has reminded me of my essence as a writer. | Joy! |
| I see the importance of this time. | Gratitude |

*There is always a way to peace, love, joy. Know that in your hearts and souls. You can always choose higher. I am with you always.*

*January 23*

Good morning, God. I haven't written in a few days. My dad was in intensive care, but he's home now and doing pretty well. He was in renal failure while in the hospital, and we thought we were losing him. I prepared to say good-bye, and it was extremely difficult for all of us. But then, he bounced back.

During this time, it was interesting to see how differently friends responded to what I was going through. A couple male friends weren't there for me at all like I'd hoped they'd be. Other friends were so caring and loving.

*Do not judge those who cannot be there for you in times of need.*

But I'd hoped they'd have responded differently.

*How?*

By calling me or asking me about my dad.

*Can they touch their own pain?*

Um…actually, both of these individuals hold walls there. I imagine the walls protect them from being deeply hurt again.

*And if they cannot touch their own pain, it would make it extremely difficult to come close to yours. You are not cut of the same fabric.*

No, it's clear that part of my work is to be a witness to people's pain and grief and to hold them through it.

*And you are able to do that with ease because you have touched the depths of your own pain with Talia's life and death, with your divorce, etc. That pain no longer scares you, so you are able to be there for another. There is more to this though that you're not seeing yet.*

There is?

*Yes. Look at both friends' earlier lives; both had deep father issues. One's father was not existent in his life, and the other's father physically and emotionally abused him. Both still hold pain around "father" energy. So for you to be going through something challenging with your father, especially since you hold a loving energy towards him, is outside the realm of what they can envision. It is a point of growth and healing for both should they choose to go there. But often that pain is deeply locked away, but it does surface in other ways.*

How?

*A need to be in control because their lives were so very much not in control. What happened to them was painful and out of their control.*

I understand that and can see how if affects their lives today. But can we get back to my dad?

*Sure. I wanted you to have the understanding—because often when a person does not have understanding, he or she tends to judge others for responses that do not fit the way that person would have liked them to respond.*

Thank you. So when my dad was in the hospital, I was confused about what to pray. And a little perplexed about what prayer can do. If it was his soul's time to transition into spirit and if my prayer was for him to get better, am I praying against what is best for him? I know that it is important for us to pray.

*Why?*

Because it helps, doesn't it?

*Who does it help, Sandy?*

It helps me, for sure.

*Good, just be clear about that.*

But wait, prayer has to help the person you're praying for.

*Yes, it does…only if they choose to accept it. Have you ever given a compliment to someone and they haven't accepted it because they don't believe it?*

Yes, and prayer is the same way? Okay, help me here. What is prayer for? Who does it help? How are we "supposed" to pray? Oh, God, I'm even scared to ask. These are bold questions for me. It was easier to ask you who the robber was in my house.

*These questions have been in your heart for some time. I'm glad you're asking them. They will help many. I'm going to keep this as simple as possible— no history, no thee's, thou's, or shalt's. I'll say this in your terms.*

*Are you ready? Prayer is the language of your thoughts. It can bring you back to who you are/who I am. It can become the compassionate language of your heart. It can be the wish of your soul put into words. Prayer can move one from the ego state to the heart state. It can turn even the most hardened heart to a soft, vulnerable place to be real. So what is prayer for? To help you to become real…to help you to remember what is real—love.*

*Who does it help? Let's break it down into prayers for you and prayers for another. First, for yourself, prayer helps you to become real, to admit that you're scared rather than hiding it underneath false pride, to admit that you feel hopeless rather than hiding it underneath frustration, to admit that you're hurt rather than hiding it underneath anger. When you acknowledge in your prayer what it is that you're really feeling, you become more real to yourself. Depending on your idea of me, you may become like a little child waiting for punishment or hoping I'll forgive you. Or you may understand that you have simply forgotten who you really are and use that awareness to let my love sink into every fiber of your being…and remember what feeling love is about. So, to pray for yourself is to realign yourself with who you really are…me. Does that make sense to you?*

Yes, absolutely. It is about remembering that we have forgotten, that we have possibly acted out of a place of being scared or hurt. So when we pray for something that we want…

*Know that you may not always get what you want. It may not be the best for you. You may know on some level that it is really not what you need, so the energy of the prayer is mixed. Like when your prayers were to attract a soul mate, a part of you knew you needed to spend time healing, writing, and becoming clear about what it is that you really want. You desired to fill a void with a relationship, but you needed to fill it in a different way first. And you did that...with me.*

Thanks. So, is it appropriate to pray for something specific? Because just praying for "my highest and best" just doesn't feel strong enough.

*Strong enough for what?*

You ask good questions.

*So do you. Strong enough for what?*

Strong enough to make something happen. It feels too...wimpy. Oh sorry, God, but it does.

*Here we are again with you trying to "make something happen," little warrior woman. You attempt to make something happen when you don't trust that the universe is on your side.*

I can feel my resistance rising up to what you're saying. I've come to understand that we can attract what we want by asking for it and holding the thought and energy of it.

*Yes, that's true.*

But now you're saying that we are supposed to pray for our "highest and best."

*Did I say that...or did you? Go back and check.*

Ha ha...I did. But, oh my god, I feel like I'm having an argument with you, God. I know I could never win!

*It's not about winning, Sandy. It never is. Nor is life ever about proving who's right and who's wrong. Religions have done a good enough job of that. But let's go back and clarify what the resistance entails. My words to you were that prayer is the language of your heart, that it can bring you into a remembrance of who you really are...love in physical form. Yes, it is good to be clear about what it is you'd like to experience on your playing field of life, but your soul has already set up circumstances for you, and aligning with that soul purpose will save you much aggravation.*

*But your tools of conscious creation are helpful because they help you to choose higher for yourselves. You and I were discussing two different uses for prayer. I was referring to prayers for you for peace. You were talking about prayers for specific tangible things. Let's break it down even further, shall we?*

*When you pray for peace within yourself, you are in a place to align with me. The only thing that keeps you from peace is yourself and old thoughts that hold you in the vibration that is not of peace. Look to the ideas you cling to about yourself. Do they reflect a God essence? If they are loving, you may pass go and collect your $200 now.*

God, you make me smile. Please continue.

*When you pray for specific material things—a specific car, a specific mate, etc.—it is a way to attract that into your life, but please do let go once you've made your request. You wouldn't follow the waitress into the kitchen to make sure she gives the request to the cook and then stand over the cook to make sure your order is correct. There is a certain level of trust there. The same is true with life.*

How about when someone prays for a relationship…or for financial turnaround?

*Let me say this—as I said before—the only thing that keeps you from peace is yourself; the only thing keeping you from a relationship or from abundance is yourself. This is **not** a judgment; it is a call to return to loving yourself even more. Your thoughts about your situation will keep you stuck there or will help you to shift your position. Your thoughts become your prayer, which becomes your reality.*

*When you pray from your heart, you will feel more of an effect from your prayer. When you pray from your heart, you remember that we are one. And in the energy of love, all things flow: financial energy, relationship energy, and creative energy.*

*Forgiveness of self is key. For if you hold yourself in judgment, you keep yourself "out of my kingdom," which plainly stated means "out of love." That **is** my kingdom. My kingdom is love. My will is love. Always. And heaven is a consciousness of love. And trespassing is acting out of a place that is not of love.*

*So, here is the Lord's Prayer translated into words that your heart may understand…*

| Our father, who art in heaven… | *God, you are the energy of love itself.* |
| Hallowed be thy name | *I allow myself to be in your presence.* |
| Thy kingdom come | *Your love is here.* |
| Thy will be done | *Let love come into my mind and my thoughts.* |
| On earth as it is in heaven. | *Right here, right now.* |
| Give us this day our daily bread. | *I trust that all is as it is meant to be.* |
| Forgive us for our trespasses | *Help me to see where I have not acted out of love.* |
| As we forgive those who trespass against us. | *Help me to not judge, but to have compassion for those who have acted out of fear or anger.* |
| And lead us not into temptation. | *Help me to recognize when there is a perceived void within me and fill it with love.* |
| But deliver us from evil. | *So that I don't act from fear or lack.* |
| For thine is the kingdom, power and glory forever. | *You are love; you are my source… forever.* |
| Amen. | *And so it is…even now.* |

*So, putting it all together…*

*God, you are the energy of love itself.*
*I allow myself to be in your presence.*
*Your love is here.*
*Let love come into my mind and my thoughts.*
*Right here, right now.*
*I trust that all is as it is meant to be.*
*Help me to see where I have not acted out of love.*
*Help me to not judge, but to have compassion for*
*those who have acted out of fear or anger.*
*Help me to recognize a perceived void within me and fill it with love.*
*So that I don't act from fear or lack.*
*You are love; you are my source…forever.*
*And so it is…even now.*

*See how that feels differently for you. It transports your energy to a higher place. So, you can see how prayer changes you?*

Yes, it does. It brings me to a softer spot in my heart.

*From there, you may choose to add your personal prayers.*

I can see how it helps the one who prays. So, can we talk about praying for another person? How does prayer help them?

*When you pray for another person, what are you praying for?*

Well, sometimes people ask me to pray for their loved one to get better. When my dad was in the hospital this last weekend, I just kept praying for peace for all involved. I think because I remember our earlier conversation that health without peace isn't worth much.

*Praying for love to be shown or for peace to be felt is the highest prayer you can pray—because peace and love are the highest vibrations that one can feel. You can pray for one's loved ones to be healed physically...*

But this is where I'm confused. Are we praying for them to be healed because we want to be out of our worry or out of our own sacredness? Oh, God, I just wrote sacredness. I meant to write scaredness.

*Interesting...because those are two ways you can pray. Out of your sacredness...or out of your scaredness. Sometimes you pray for a certain outcome so that you won't feel a certain way...or so that you won't feel a sense of loss. That is out of a place of scaredness.*

Like when people pray, "Please let me win the lottery, so that I can pay off the debt"?

*Yes. Not a very effective prayer, by the way. Other times, you pray from your sacredness when you pray that you or another individual will remember truth, remember love.*

Like "God, I know that you are abundance, and I know that I am a part of you. Help me to heal the thoughts I'm holding that keep me in financial lack."

*Exactly. See the difference?*

Yes! One tries to get a quick fix, and the other helps shift the energy within you, so that you can live from a higher vibration.

*When you pray, "God, please help me to get out of this mess I am in," it would help you more in the long run to open your heart and affirm, "God, help me to heal the thoughts that got me into this mess."*

I can see how different that would feel.

*Let me shed some light on what prayer can do for another. You can never override the soul's wish. The soul is the powerful energy of who you are…it is one with my energy. If you pray for another and hold a vision of their healing, their soul must be in agreement with it. When many hold a vision for another, when you have many individuals praying for the same individual, you hold a higher vibration for that individual, which they may not know how to do on their own. You pray for a potential. As long as the soul agrees, the body will heal. I am not the one deciding which prayers are answered. You are. Remember my will is love.*

Oh, so back to "free will-y"…were you trying to tell me to free "love"?

*You got it. Love is within all. Free it…let it out. And love frees all from the bonds of hurt, hate, anger, and pain.*

Cool! So I don't have to go and rent the movie after all?

*No, you don't. And hopefully this will shed light for many others. So many believe that I answer specific prayers and allow certain healing to happen but hold back at other times.*

I know. It's not you doing it.

*No, why would I play favorites? You are all part of me, and I am part of you.*

So, can we recap this whole idea of prayer? Prayer changes us. Prayer can help another if their soul agrees to it.

*Yes, but I need to add one more thing here. When you hear a loving compliment from another and you receive it, it feels good to you, right? And it can help you to remember that you are lovable.*

Yes.

*So, think of praying for another in this way. When you hold someone in an energy of affection and light, you send them vibrations of love, which are like warm blankets of love, which can melt through much of the iciness of fear and worry. So, do you want to hear the most powerful prayer of all?*

Definitely.

*Three simple words. I love you. From the heart, I love you. It is actually the highest prayer you can utter. I love you. Say it to yourself, say it to your children, say it to your friends and your parents, and yes, you can even say it to me, but all forms of it are like saying it to yourself.*

How come we didn't just go there from the beginning when I asked about prayer?

*Because inquiring minds needed to know. Your mind likes the detail. I like to make it quite simple.*

So, I love you. That's it. That's the highest prayer? What about thy will be done?

*It is the same thing. Love will be done here...love is present here...I am a conduit for love...I love you. Where many of you have a tendency to get in trouble is that those three words hold such a charged emotional energy and can bring all kinds of attachments and expectations with it. We'll talk about that in a minute. Your brain is full. Go take a break.*

Thanks, I was just thinking that my eyes are getting a little buggy. I'm going to go make some tea and some breakfast and get my reading glasses. Hey, God...I love you.

*I love you too.*

~~~~~

I'm back.

*I'm still here.*

I can see clearly now. My glasses are on.

*Sandy, you all can see clearly whenever you remember truth. When you begin to see truth, you cannot pretend anymore. And many of you are pretending. You all are being called to a higher level of vibration...to the essence of love. Wherever you cling to fear, you will often draw the very fear to you—not because you are bad or stupid, but so that you may look at the fear, to neutralize it. In other words, you see it for what it really is with "neutral eyes" and remember that it cannot really harm or destroy you.*

*When you realize that there is never anything to fear, you come to a fuller and deeper realization of love. It all comes back to love. No matter how far you stray, no matter what you do, love is there.*

So, can we go back to what we talked about before...about saying "I love you"? That is such a scary concept for many people. It wasn't spoken often in our family, but we knew we were loved.

*One can easily say "I'm sleepy" or "I'm thirsty." But there is something about the words "I love you" that causes fear to rear up. Some are comfortable with "love you" or "love ya," but the words...I...love...you...well, that's something different. Let's look at it. What fears do you imagine surround those words?*

The first thing that comes to mind is...what if the person doesn't say it back? Ugh, I've been there, not just with romantic partners but with friends and family members. It has made me feel vulnerable and stupid at times, thinking, "Oh, they don't feel the same about me." It has saddened me in the past.

*Good, very good, and you felt sad because...*

I think because I wanted the other person to love me. But it can also depend on where I am emotionally when I say it. Sometimes, I like to say it to someone because it is just what I'm feeling. Other times, I need to hear it back, and when I don't, I feel less than.

*Less than what?*

Less than loved.

*By them?*

Yes, by them.

*Let's bring truth to this picture. Someone's ability to say "I love you" really has nothing to do with who you are, but with what they are feeling. You just said it. Learn to say it as a statement, not in the form of a question, looking for a response.*

I'm a little confused. How do I ever say it as a question?

*When you say, "I'm so sleepy," you're not looking to another person to say, "I'm so sleepy too." You simply state what you feel, right?*

Yes.

*Let "I love you" be the same. Rather than searching for another person to affirm you by saying it back, let it be a statement of what you feel.*

But what if "I love you" pushes people away because they think that I have ulterior motives.

*Do you?*

No…well, sometimes, maybe. Ugh, maybe if I'm feeling a little insecure, I may need to hear it back to make me feel better, and if I don't hear it, I feel worse.

*So, if you do have an ulterior motive, it would be good to look at it and acknowledge what you're really feeling. A concealed purpose usually signals a void that is trying to be filled. If there isn't one there, then you are not responsible for someone's discomfort level for love.*

God, what about my friend who said recently to me, "You have to use those words 'I love you' sparingly because they are so powerful."

*They **are** tremendously powerful. But would you withhold love from someone because it is powerful?*

No.

*Sandy, when people hear "I love you," they may not be listening to the actual words, but may be hearing what they imagine that you mean. People fall into their past or project into the future with those words, rather than feeling the energy of the words in the present moment.*

That makes sense to me.

*You have found that you can love people in different ways. You can appreciate different aspects of people and tell them that you love them. Some people hear "I love you" but don't feel the energy of love in the moment, but rather they feel "hooks" digging into them, which is from their fear. "I love you" doesn't mean "I own you." It also does not mean "I will be with you forever." It means "who I am in this moment, loves who you are in this moment." Truly, there is no other moment outside the present one anyway.*

I like that. Does it also mean, "I love what I feel when I am with you"?

*Not really. If that is what you feel, say it too.*

Can you say "I love you" to someone when you love parts of them and there may be other parts of them that you don't love? Or should you wait to say it until you love all parts of them?

*If you wait, you may be waiting a lifetime. Have you ever truly loved all parts of a person?*

No…well, maybe in the infatuation stage, when you don't feel anything else but the warm fuzzies.

*The question really is…have you ever truly loved all parts of yourself? Because the more you can love all parts of yourself, the more you will be able to love all parts of another.*

I have to laugh because I'm thinking back to prior relationships… little things that I'd *love* about a person (like the way he chews… "ooh, it's so cute how he eats that…") later on could become something I couldn't stand!

*Yes, that happens. But let's return to this idea of loving all parts. It would be more beneficial for you to see the person as a whole…rather than parts. You may never find yourself in a relationship with someone whom you love all parts of. Look to the whole. Appreciate what is there. We are talking about two different things: saying "I love you" in a romantic relationship and saying "I love you" to a friend or acquaintance. When you say "I love you" to a friend, it's easier for you because you may not know about all their quirks that appear when they're not with you, and you certainly don't have to live with it. But when you add the romantic element, the scrutiny is there. You have seen it with your former husband. The love you have for him now is different than it was when you were married to him, isn't it?*

Yes, it has become a deep compassion that will always be there.

*That is beautiful…and perfect for the two of you. You have not allowed your differences to keep you apart. Job well done for all hearts involved. Compassion is a high vibration of energy. Your world would be a brighter place if more people felt it. But many stay in relationships long after the purpose has been served. Resentment builds, and compassion is nowhere to be found.*

God, I feel like I truly love so many people.

*And you tell them, don't you?*

Yes, many of them…even my clients. My prayer before they come in is usually, "God, help me to just love this person right where they are."

*And what does that do for you?*

It softens my heart and opens me up for guidance in a powerful way.

*And it enables you to love the person as they are, as you are, without looking for them to be a certain way. Brilliant! Imagine if you did that with every person that you crossed paths with, not just your clients. Imagine if more people did that…brought their attention to love first. "Help me to love this person right where they are. This is at the heart of the words, "Love thy neighbor as thyself."*

Here we go with the "thy's." Oh, I'm sorry…you know I mean no disrespect by that.

*I can take your humor, Sandy. Use this day as an experiment.*

Rut roh…more homework.

*As you move through your day, hold the thought, "Let me love this person right where they are." As you go through Dunkin Donuts to get your coffee…as you go into your office building…with your children…at your son's basketball practice tonight…on the phone, hold these thoughts for one day, "Let me love this person right where they are." And will you report back tomorrow?*

Will do. I feel pressure now. I hope I can remember. I'll start with my dog, Mikey. Will it work with him too?

*What do you think?*

I know it will. This will be fun. I'll report back at 0600 tomorrow.

*You're silly. And, Sandy, have fun with it.*

I will. Thanks, God, I love you.

*I love you too.*

*February 25*

God, so much has happened since I last wrote. I don't know if I ever completed the homework that you assigned. Maybe I did it for a couple hours. I just can't remember.

*Sandy, your heart has been through much. Go easy on yourself.*

My dad had been in and out of the hospital and ended up coming home from the hospital at about five p.m. on January 31. We arranged to have him start with hospice the next day. God, he looked so cute when the medics brought him home. He wasn't doing too well physically, but we thought he knew he was home, and he seemed happy about it. And we were glad to have him home. My poor mom was tired. So many trips to the hospital, so many unknowns—it seemed to be taking a toll on her.

My sisters had set up the living room with a hospital bed, and the room looked very comfortable. We didn't know how long we had left with my dad. We thought maybe three months or six months. It was hard to know what to expect.

I had decided to sleep at my parents' house that night and so did my sister Penny to help my mom with anything she'd need for Dad on his first night there. We also hired a home health aide to help with his care for the first night.

After dinner, he was starting to get pretty restless. He kept asking to get out of bed, but we couldn't let him because he had virtually no strength left. Though, I'm not even sure at that point he even knew what he was saying.

We called hospice, and they came at eleven that night. They started him on morphine and another drug to help calm him. My mom looked exhausted, so we told her to go to bed. At five a.m., I woke up because I heard some noises in the living room. When I went out there, I looked at my dad and then at the home health aide...and knew. My dad had died about fifteen minutes prior. My mom and my sister then woke up...and we hugged each other, hugged my dad, and cried. Then it was time to call the other sisters. Thankfully, they all live within fifteen minutes of my parents' home and were there with their kids quickly. I called Rich, who also came and brought my kids.

It was hard saying good-bye. It was difficult to watch my mom hold Dad's face, hug him, place her head on his chest, and cry. It was hard to watch my kids and my nieces and nephews say their good-byes to Papa. He was such a good man—a well-loved man. It's going to be a long journey for my mom. They were married for fifty-six years. As sad as it was, there was so much love in the room. I am so grateful for my family. Thank you, God.

The day after he died, my sisters and I were at my mom's house, and I kept feeling his presence around me. I asked my sisters and mom if we could all go into the living room because I felt Daddy wanted to talk to us. So we all got comfy on my mom's couches in the sunny living room... and my dad was right there, sending me his thoughts. He kept saying, "I love you, I love you, I love you, I love you, I love you, and I love you." (He said an "I love you" for each of us.)

My dad was not a verbal "I-love-you" kind of person. We knew he loved us by his actions and how he gave, but "I love you" did not flow easily from his lips. And what his spirit essence "said" to me was this, "It's easy to say 'I love you' now because I'm sending you the **thoughts**... and you're able to hear them. I thought those words so often when I was there physically, but the words got stuck **here**" (he pointed to his heart and throat).

*Sandy, so many in physical form have thoughts that get stuck, and they cannot verbalize what they'd like to. It is all okay . It is part of your learning. Interestingly, so many of you do not trust my love or feel that it is enough; if you did, there would be more peace on your earth. Soon, many will learn to perceive thoughts of God/Spirit and know that love more readily. On your physical level, the spoken word has become more important than thought. But how would one hear my voice other than thought. So to all who are reading these words, hear my thoughts as you read this: "I LOVE YOU."*

God, thank you for inspiring me to write something and share it at my dad's service. I really felt your presence within me as I read it, and I know it touched many hearts.

*So share it now...*

Ok, this is what I wrote with your help.

~~~~~~~~~~

Imagine if we all had a conversation with God before we came here to earth to get our assignment...our mission, if you will. I imagine this is the conversation that God had with my dad before he arrived here.

*Ok, Zarven, you ready to go to earth?*

Sure, God, what's my mission there?

*Well, it's pretty simple. You're there to love.*

That's it?

*Yes...to love.*

How do I love?

*Many can do it through words, but we want you to show it through your actions. Your actions will speak louder than words.*

Okay, sounds easy enough. Who am I to love?

*Well, first we're going to match you up with a most beautiful woman who will become your loving companion for fifty-six years.*

Wow, fifty-six years. Won't we tire of each other after all that time?

*Oh, Zarven. You don't understand what love is yet, but you will. And no, you won't ever tire of each other. Your love will deepen right to the very end.*

Okay, so how will I know her?

*You'll meet her at a beach party, tell her you love her after the third date, and ask her to marry you after your sixth date.*

Why so soon?

*Because she will be the one to bear your children.*

I'll have children there on earth?

God laughs and says, *Oh yes…you'll have a girl.*

Oh, good.

*Well, actually, you'll have more than one girl.*

That's fine…girls are great.

*Well, actually, you'll have five girls.*

Five girls? How many bathrooms does that come with?

*One.*

One?

*Yes, one, and you will never complain.*

Whatever you say, God. You're the boss.

*And to support all these kids, you'll work hard your whole life, and you'll enjoy it too. You'll earn money, but it won't be the most important thing to you. You'll use it to take pleasure in life. Got it?*

Got it. Sounds like fun. Can you put me in yet?

*No. There are some things you'll need to remember while you're there. You won't preach about love, you'll show it through your actions. You'll be a great provider, a loving husband, caring father, proud papa to thirteen grandchildren, a wonderful boss, and a great encourager to many.*

Wow, what a nice guy I get to be…

*Yes, and, Zarven, you'll never ask for anything in return.*

Nothing? But it sounds like I'll be doing so much for other people. I don't get anything in return?

*I didn't say you won't **get** anything in return. I said you'll never **ask** for anything in return. Your mission there is to serve others. And in return, you'll receive the greatest gift of all.*

What's that?

*Love. You will be loved by all who know you—by your wife, your daughters, your sons-in-law, your grandchildren…and they'll tell two friends who'll love you, and they'll tell two friends and so on. Deal or no deal?*

Deal! But how will I remember all of this?

*I'll give you a little instruction booklet that will tell you all that you need to remember. It only contains four simple instructions: live fully; give freely; show your love; appreciate life now. But there's no place for you to carry this little instruction booklet…so I'm placing it in your heart.*

So, Zarven Alemian took on his earthly body and did as he was told. He lived fully, he gave freely, he showed his love, and he appreciated life to the fullest. And now I imagine the conversation that my dad would have with God as he sheds his body and returns to God….

How did I do, God? How did I do on earth?

*Job well done, Zarven, mission accomplished. Now it is up to all of them to remember that I've place those same instructions in their hearts as well… your youngest one is delivering the message right now.*

So, to all of you who are hearing this today, who may have known my dad directly or through one of us, may you remember that you have those same instructions in your heart as well. May you give without seeking anything in return; and in return, may you receive the greatest gift of all….LOVE.

*February 26*

God, it's been a few weeks now, and I know my dad is alright in spirit...that he is relieved to be out of his body. We've had signs from him, but it's an interesting journey to walk, knowing what we know about Spirit, connecting with him in Spirit, and yet still having to traverse the physical path of grief at the same time. I miss the physical presence of my dad. I'm functioning really well...some around me are surprised. But when I stop doing, I feel it all—what a concept. It's what you told me at the very start of this book—to stop doing so much. I can see now why I resisted it.

*Allow the feelings to come up, dear one. Do not run from what you feel. That is what you have done in your past: distracted yourself, busy-ed yourself— all to avoid on a subconscious level that which you choose not to feel.*

I felt it all yesterday; the weight of my emotions came crashing down on me when I went for a walk in the woods. I started sobbing, and I couldn't stop. An intense sadness (that I hadn't felt in such a long time) pierced through me. I felt an extreme emotional tiredness and total confusion. Why am I here? Does anything matter anymore? Am I really making a difference here? I felt like I was done trying, done with all the "doing." I felt like my soul was deciding, "Should I stay or should I go?" It has happened to me a couple times before: once right after Talia died and once after my divorce. It wasn't a physical tiredness...but an emotional and spiritual one. I was breaking apart inside.

*Sandy, good for you for allowing yourself to feel it. These instances were breakdowns on some level...and often signal that a breakthrough is about to occur. Old layers, old patterns are being broken. You may have felt the pieces of your life around you, but you weren't sure what to do with them or how anything fit anymore.*

Yes, and it was scary.

*Breakthroughs often can be because one is asked to allow an old energetic pattern to be free, and it can leave you vulnerable and naked. Calling your friend was the right thing to do.*

Yes, my friend Michael's face kept coming to my mind. He's been a spiritual mentor for me, and I knew he would be able to help me see this with clarity. Thank you for Michael, God; he is such a bright light to so many. Thank you for his willingness to be a vehicle here for truth, for love, and for compassion.

*All are called to be that vehicle, Sandy, not all answer the call.*

Michael helped me to see the similarities between my divorce and my dad's death. Both have been opportunities to nudge me to grow—to let go of what is familiar, what is known. And rather than cling to what was, I am to stand in the present moment...and be and feel...and trust that I will be led. This lesson occurs with striking importance for me and for friends around me: this concept of being in the moment and allowing you, God, and life to move me in the moment.

*Great concept, isn't it?*

Yes, but it brings up so much fear! Because when you're not planning, not doing, not knowing, and not controlling the environment around you, anything can happen.

*And your point is...*

If anything can happen, how will you know what you're going to have to feel?

*So, you are only willing to feel certain things? Or you fear experiencing certain emotions and so then you avoid feeling them?*

93

Ugh…yes, here we go again. But no one wants to feel pain, disappointment….

*Because what if they do…*

It hurts.

*And what happens when you hurt? You begin to decide some things about yourself, right? "That was stupid. How did I let that happen again; I should've known better…" All those are unneeded judgments. Let yourself feel the discomfort and breathe with it. Breathe into it…and you will realize that it doesn't last. Look at how you felt less than twenty-four hours ago and now feel the peace in your heart. No feelings last, Sandy, don't avoid them. They won't kill you. But not feeling them can contribute to many physical ailments that humans experience: tightness of chest, digestive issues, headaches, dis-eases. Let go of the judgments on feelings and let them be. Be with them.*

I'm learning how to do that, but I have to tell you when I have a feeling of anxiety rise up, sometimes it's easier to run from it…to tell it to go away…or want to blame someone else for making me feel that way.

*And has that worked?*

Not really, it may disappear, but I think the more accurate way to describe it is that the feelings go underground. And that affects how I relate to others.

*So let's look at that…how your underground emotions influence how you relate with others.*

Okay.

*First, let's clarify how emotions go underground. Often one does not want to feel them because of what they have experienced in the past…which was not resolved. The emotion leaves them remembering a past trigger that is still an open wound. Following so far?*

I think so. So an emotion that we don't want to feel is a trigger that there is a wound that we don't want to touch?

*Yes. And in order to avoid that wound, one denies the feeling that would lead them there. How many men recently have told you that they care about you but are afraid of getting hurt again?*

More than I'd like to admit.

*So they "run from love" because in their past, experiencing love led them to pain, which they are now trying to avoid. It is not love they are evading… it is pain. So, if it is pain or rather their unhealed wound they avoid, they've assumed that love will lead to their wound. Your friend said to you the other day that he was afraid to let people near his heart.*

Yes, and I told him (inspired by you) that maybe it was more like he was afraid to let people near his **hurt.** Why are we so afraid to be with our pain…to let others see our hurt…to let others near us? We tend to isolate; I know I do. Why do we do that?

*Hopefully, in isolation, you will give yourselves an opportunity to remember that I am always with you. Some will feel it…some won't. Not because they can't but because they won't, which is a big difference. Not all are willing to feel my love, Sandy.*

I know that, but why not?

*Some have been taught that I am a God to be feared. Most do not love what they fear. Others have been taught that I am a punishing God, which instills more terror. And others may have had their first experiences of what love was supposed to be come from parents who didn't have love to give or who filtered love through anger or through harshness because it is what they knew. So early experiences or expectations of what was called "love" hurt.*

How can we help those who feel that way? I questioned a friend of mine just yesterday, "What if we only knew that God's love was enough?" We so often try to be loved by outside things and people, who can only love us the way they were taught or do the best they can through their own filters. Why don't we trust you, God? Why don't we know that your love is enough?

*So many questions this morning, little one, so many why's. Why don't **you** trust me? What keeps you from knowing that my love is enough for **you**?*

This is the crux of it, isn't it? Let me feel my way into this; I haven't trusted you because I didn't really know you.

*Excellent start.*

95

And I didn't really know you because I didn't spend time getting acquainted with you. I have placed more trust in the humanness of people in my life than I have in you. You are non-physical, God, so I think it has been easier to place my faith and trust in that which I can see. Ugh.

Funny, though, this dialog is becoming a very physical thing, isn't it? I'm making it a physical object by putting your thoughts to paper. There's more to that; I can sense it. But I want to finish with these thoughts. I have been attached to "proof"…to "achievements"…to the tangible things here. That's why I think I haven't trusted you. Anything I've missed?

*Sandy, many will identify with these words. And yes, there is more to what you were sensing. But please answer the question, "What gets in the way of knowing that my love isn't enough for you?"*

I'm not sure if I know, but I have imagined what your love is like. It's crazy because whenever I feel my connection to you, whether it is through meditation or writing, I am filled with such a sense of completeness—there is nothing missing. It is enough, overflowing actually. So, I do have moments of knowing that your love is enough.

*Maybe the question is "Why do you so infrequently choose to remember that it is enough?"*

I think you're right. My answer is….the distractions, the busy-ness, the trying to achieve…

*And I am with you even through all of that, but your focus is elsewhere. You have had times when you're driving on the highway, and you've driven past the exit you were meant to take, right?*

Yes.

*Did the exit go away? Or were you just distracted, thinking of something else?*

Ha ha. You're right.

*It's not about being right…it's about what is so. Think about this: On the highway of life, I am always with you, though your "driven-ness" can distract you.*

Ooh, I like that! And we drive by like you're not even there.

*And you drive like I'm not even in the car with you.*

Are we going to talk about my driving? Because I know I drive too fast and talk on my cell phone.

*And why do you do that?*

Because of this "hurry up and fit it all in" thread that has run through my life.

*And what do you imagine would happen if you didn't accomplish it all? No one dies with it all done, Sandy. And there is no place to get to. It is all about the journey.*

I have to breathe. This is a major lesson for me that has been with me for all my life. Slow down…let it be…what gets done, gets done.

*And if it takes four trips to the car to get all the groceries instead of two… so what? You even load yourself up with too many grocery bags, little one. And you wonder why you are tired. What do you imagine would happen if you slowed down and had the courage to do less?*

I'd have more time to connect with you. Oh my God. This is all I think I ever really wanted. Maybe my endless search in this lifetime was to really know you, to really know your voice, your love. I want to cry. "Looking for love in all the wrong places…" is the song I hear in my head right now.

*Be with this, Sandy. It is not only what your endless search has been about…but it is the endless search for many in this lifetime. Be with this. Feel the implications of it. Acknowledge the simplicity of it all.*

I feel as if I just was pummeled between the eyes—with a truth that I've been looking for all my life. How could I not have known this? How do I stay in tune with it; I don't want to keep forgetting, God. It's too painful to forget.

*It matters not how many times you forget, little one. I'm always here; you can always remember one more time.*

Remembering one more time—I like that. What I just sensed too is that no matter where our journeys take us…perhaps it all comes back to remembering your love. It's so simple, yet not always so easy.

*No matter how far you stray, how deep you are in your sleepiness, how much "failure" you witness in your life, no matter how much you believe you have made a "mess" of it all, no matter how angry you become at the world or at yourself, no matter why you don't know my love, in the "end," it doesn't really matter. And this can be the "end"—the "end" of your pain, the "end" of your struggle, the "end" of your search. END: **E**go **N**ear **D**eath.*

We don't need the ego?

*If you think of EGO in the common way. It is referred to in your human terms as Easing God Out. It would be good to call an end to that, no?*

Wow…so cool.

*It is the end of easing God/love out. Or simply put…it is letting God/love back in. It is a wakeup call for many to live differently. Many are tired of the pain, tired of the struggle.*

Perhaps the pain was needed to fuel the struggle, which would then lead them to searching…which would ultimately lead them to love, hopefully.

*I am at every stop along the way. I am with them during the pain; I am with them during the struggle; I am with them during the search. Always. Some need to go through it for the experience.*

*March 14*

God, I feel very unsettled right now. I keep hearing from friends and clients about all that they put up with in life. They say "it's okay" when it's really not. When a spouse swears at them or doesn't support them… or when they tolerate work or anyone in their life that is, in their words, "Sucking the very life out of them." How have we allowed that to be the norm? It does not honor our divine essence.

*But it may be very "normal" to them.*

I want to help to alleviate that here, God, to let people know that it's not okay to be treated like that by anyone…that they don't have to settle.

*Breathe, little one, breathe. You have been there yourself…and remember that not all is as it seems.*

What do you mean?

*It is not all bad for them. For instance, the woman who said that her job is sucking the life out of her, what is it giving back to her?*

She said it is giving her an income that she needs.

*So it is offering her something.*

Yes, but it is "killing her" in her words. But she is afraid to leave because she believes that job is the only source of income for her.

*And your friends whose husbands are "sucking the life right out of them," what do these men give to them?*

Their husbands provide them with financial security that they are afraid to be without.

*So staying in the situation helps them to divert themselves from facing what they truly fear. They've made it a black and white game, a clever little game that you all play, so as not to feel the fear—to not feel what you sense you will lose. "I will stay in this relationship that is not healthy for me…because without it, I will be destitute, I will be alone." It is just fear. Let's look at the fear that rears up and what behaviors/actions people take to avoid confronting that fear. In other words,* **actions** *have become* **"distr-actions"** *from fear.*

Ooh, this is going to be good.

*The fear that comes up is…"this person, this job, this relationship, this home…fill in the blank…is the SOURCE of what will sustain me." Is that truth?*

No.

*But it is what you have come to believe. You see that a particular person, a job, a relationship, or a home is the form in which blessings happen to be flowing to you. Do not attach to the form…blessings flow no matter what. Imagine if you were in front of a running stream of water and were extremely thirsty. Imagine someone came to you and offered you a bottle to fill so that you could drink the water. You could become attached to the person who brought you the bottle.*

Right. We'd say, "No! don't leave me! You brought me this bottle; you saved me…I *need* you."

*What you don't know is that there are many who could potentially bring you that bottle. And you could attach yourself to the bottle itself. But what is truly the sustenance here is the water. So many of you emotionally rely upon the form and believe that the form is the source of what fills you. You also believe that without this person, this job, or this thing, that you are nothing.*

You are the source, aren't you?

*I am. That I am.*

And without the other person, job, or thing, we could always be whole.

*Yes…but one may have to face that fear of nothingness to realize that they could be whole. Take the woman who is dedicated to a job she hates but stays because of the money. The job is not the source of income; it is the form through which abundance currently flows. At any time, she can choose to remember that abundance is a steady stream of energy and flows to her right now in the form of income in the form of her current job. But **at what price** is she willing to hold on to her old beliefs, especially since it affects her physically with all the stress and the toxicity due to her clinging to her hate of her job?*

*And for your friends, what price are they willing to pay in order to wake up to their own self worth, self-respect? Please do not judge anyone here; you've all been there, staying in a situation because for whatever reason you don't want to examine the fear that freezes you there. As you look at the fear, you realize that it is not real…though it most certainly feels like it is. When you experience it, sit with it, and remember that I am with you, even in the midst of your worst fear, the terror begins to dissipate, and you can transmute any energy. You will also be able to recognize and identify the self-destructing behaviors that you engage in, in order to not feel the fear.*

We do that, don't we?

*Yes, you do…until you remember something.*

What?

*Love.*

Love?

*Yes, love. When you love yourself, love your essence, you choose healthier ways of treating yourself. Love doesn't ridicule, love doesn't hurt another, love heals, and love speaks truth with love. But what has happened is that people have fallen "out of love" with themselves first and then have seen that reflected in their workplaces or in their relationships. It is a call to return to love. Yes, it is that plain and simple. Love.*

So, how can they start?

*By being with what is…be with the fear…and let love meet them there. They must cultivate a willingness to feel love once again…not from another.*

*This is not to be "out-sourced." This is an inside job. Love heals all. You've all paid a high enough price for it. And the truth is…it never really was meant to cost you anything. You chose to pay for it. My love is free and free flowing. What is really at the heart of it all, Sandy, is the willingness to remember love.*

And there truly is nothing to fear, is there?

*Nothing at all.*

Not financial ruin, not heartbreak, not even death.

*Not even death—there is always something on the other side of it all… and something with you through it all…*

You.

*Yes.*

Thank you, God. I want to live my life as a blessing to others…to live these words, not just write them. I know that in order for me to do that, I need to spend time in quiet moments to remember truth, to recall love, to cultivate that peacefulness that is there any time I have the courage to do less. That peace is there every time I face my desire to fill my space with another person. I guess my price to pay is confronting the fear that there may be some things that I don't accomplish today. So what if they aren't completed? I'm also aware that as I spend time in quiet, peace-filled moments (and don't rush to fill my empty moments with a man), that it doesn't mean I'll be alone forever.

Thank you for the clarity in this moment. I love you. And for the first time in a long time, I don't need to hear it back.

*You are beginning to realize that in true giving, you are also receiving.*

*March 21*

God, here I am this morning, having taken some time off from writing. I cannot believe the peace that I feel when I begin again. I have to laugh because I know better. I know the piece that is missing when I don't write. Ugh!

*Sandy, many people feel that they are missing some pieces to their lives. They lack peace. As for those that are the closest to you, you have been sensing that you are all going through a shift at the same time, correct?*

Yes, is there something more to that?

*You are part of a soul group that has decided to come back together in this lifetime to share and help one another. It is appropriate, and the circle will grow larger.*

I'm not sure I know what you mean by that.

*You don't need to know…simply trust, little one. Let's talk about the piece that many feel is missing. All will come to that piece through a different path… usually frustration leads the way. But the trail that each of you journeys on will be different. Do not judge another's path, for you have most likely walked them all at one point or another in other lifetimes. Each of you holds the space for what you believe is lacking, looking to find that missing piece (peace). For you, Sandy, you search for the relationship piece (peace). For others, it is a financial piece (peace)…and yet others it is the career piece (peace)…are you seeing the common denominator?*

Yes, we all seek peace.

*You look for it, but many push it away at the same time.*

How do we do that?

*Through your actions, through your words, you say you want it, but your actions speak louder than your words. Is what you're doing leading you into peace….or away from it? Is what you're thinking leading you into peace…or away from it? This is not a judgment on any of you, but the hope of bringing you back home…to peace. Take a timeout now.*
*Stop.*
*Just stop.*
*Just stop for a moment.*
*Breathe.*
*Stay right here with me. Right here. Right here. Breathe. Breathe. Breathe. It is all okay. I know of your struggle, and I love you anyway. I know of your hurt, your pain, and I love you anyway. I know of your fear, of your shame, of how you feel every time you forget peace and want to berate yourself for it, and I love you anyway. I hear your cries of "I don't know if I can do this anymore!"*
*So stop doing it and feel. Stop and breathe. Yes, right now. Put this book down and breathe. Put down the worries just for a moment; put down the fears and sit with me. This is a gift for you, a moment of silence for you, a moment that holds the potential of peace. Accept it. Breathe it in. Be still and know I am with you.*

That is what it takes, isn't it? Being in a moment. I actually stopped typing and sat; it felt good. How many people do you think really put this book down though?

*Numbers don't matter to me. If only one did and felt a moment of peace, the ripple effect would have a wonderful impact on this planet.*

God, this morning as I wrote in my journal, I heard these words from an old song: "Every time you go away, you take a piece of me with you." I used to joke that the words were "Every time you go away, you take a piece of **meat** with you." But this morning, I thought of you. Every time we go away from you, you are with us.

*Yes, and every time you go away, you can take my peace with you.*

I love that. Imagine if more of us brought your peace to our workplaces, to our children, to our relationships. We need to feel it first in order to take it with us though, right?

*I'm not crazy about that word "need." It implies "or else." You don't NEED to feel peace; it is a choice—one that is within the hearts of so many at this time. Choose it. See how your life shifts because of it.*

Thank you God, I really do need to get ready for the office. And I'm taking your peace with me. You're the best.

~~~~~

I'm back, God. I had a good day at the office. Today is the first day of spring, though there's still some snow on the ground, and it's a little cool out. What a difference I feel in terms of my inner confidence when I connect with you first and experience that peace first.

*Sandy, it would be like trying to run a marathon with no training: Your muscles would be sore, and you'd want to give up.*

Which many of us do, God, in different moments. Because this journey here can be so hard and confusing at times.

*It is simpler than you're all making it out to be. You hold on to so much "stuff" that is no longer needed, right? Think back to when you cleaned out your hall closet recently.*

Ugh, are we really going to talk about my closet? Well, I was pretty amazed at all the junk that was there. I knew I kept throwing stuff in there…framed pictures from past relationships, mittens that had no partners, jackets that the kids had outgrown. And each time the kids or I would open the closet to get a jacket, I'd hope that all the riffraff wouldn't tumble out, but it would. It took me growing fed up with how it looked in order to clean it out.

*Perfectly said. How many people wait until their inner pain and turmoil is "bad enough" in order to do a "life-cleansing?" But when you start the process, it doesn't always look pretty right away, does it?*

NO! In fact, when I took everything out of the closet, oh my god, I piled tons of stuff in the hallway…it looked so much worse and started to feel so overwhelming that I wanted to quit.

*But you didn't.*

No, I didn't, and eventually, I straightened it all out. Some stuff I threw away. Who needs fifteen wooden shimmies? (I'm not even sure that is the right word for them, and I wouldn't even know what to do with them!) There were unmatched mittens (maybe they are cousins to the unmatched socks that are in the basement?); there were ripped gift bags from Christmas. Some stuff I brought downstairs and some I put back neatly. And it did feel good…at the end. But while it was going on, I wasn't really enjoying the process.

*No one said it was supposed to be fun, but could something have made it more pleasant?*

Sure, now that I think about it, music always makes me smile.

*So, don't feel like you need to be miserable during these times of shifting for you. Go easy, go gentle, and know that you are loved. And you may want to keep those closets clean for your own sake…not mine.*

*April 3*

Good morning, God. So much has transpired since I last wrote. It seems like the lesson I'm working on is letting go. It relates to a man that I recently dated. We deeply felt a spiritual connection for the last couple of months. He's still processing sadness from his divorce and is not in the same place of readiness for a relationship as I am. I feel that I need to let go of him, and it saddens me.

*What do you imagine you are really releasing?*

My idea of what I thought we could share together—also expectations, attachments, and trying to arrange get-togethers with him.

*And how has the process gone for you?*

It hasn't been an easy process. Sometimes I feel like I am letting go of the very thing that sustains me.

*And is it truly sustaining you?*

No. It is what has fed my ego, but not my soul.

*What feeds your soul is not outside of you.*

Yes, that is what I am realizing.

*So what have you let go of really? How do you "let go" of an attachment or an expectation? Are they things to tangibly release?*

No, they are ideas, thoughts that held me in a place that wasn't peaceful.

*Were they holding you there? Or were you trapping yourself there?*

Ok, I was holding onto them, and by clinging to them, I wasn't feeling peace.

*So each time you release an external expectation or attachment, what happens to you?*

Well, if I'm honest, I have to recognize that a part of me doesn't want to let go...because of fear. The fear is if I let go of my attachment to this person, he'll go away all together. I want him to care about me the same way I care about him. But it's not in my control.

I do know that I am always okay, no matter who chooses to love me, or not. And what is odd is that as our relationship shifts, he is still here, and I am learning to love unconditionally.

*Do you know why?*

I'm guessing that it has to do with remembering you first, God?

*That is it. When you allow yourself to remember love first from the Source, you have it to give, and you allow yourself to give it freely without needing to receive it back...because you have so much to give. You are learning that you fill within first...not fill from the outside. Because others on the outside can only love you through their own filters (meaning, their own ability to give, which you know has nothing to do with you). Some people have filters that only permit a trickle of love to flow. Others, who are God-centered, are able to allow a greater flow of love to move through them. You all know the difference. Do not judge another for how they are able to love...or not. Simply recognize that they are in the flow...or not.*

I am realizing that and not taking it so personal anymore. But I did have to separate myself in order to remember it.

*Did you separate yourself...or did you take quiet time to remember?*

I did both, actually.

*Watch how you use that word "separate," Sandy. So many feel that they need to separate, to cut the ties from another...in order to remember divine*

love. You felt that within your marriage. But you can never really be separate…
you only can in your mind. And the physical separation that many feel they
need is only in the smaller picture. In the larger picture, you are never separate.
You are all one. You are beginning to feel that.*

Yes, I am.

*And know this, to **realize** is to see something different…to make "real"…
to see with "**real eyes.**"*

That is cute! Thank you. I'd like your insight on something. My dear
friend Peter sent me this message in an email today:
"Each moment of my life is a new moment. I live it, and then I say
good-bye for now….then I say hello to a new moment; I live it and then
say good-bye for now or at least I try to live that way. I have no idea where
anything in my life is supposed to go, but I do trust and have faith that
if I let it go with love, it will end up where it is supposed to be. And my
journey will be all that it is supposed to be."

Can you comment on it?

*The essence of it is about being in the moment. The not knowing, the trust,
and faith that life is always moving you to where you are to be. Truth. Let's
look at the idea of "letting go with love." When you let go out of anger, out of
hatred, or out of fear, are you really letting go or are you looking away? The
energy that brought you there is still there…only you choose to not look at it.
This is not a judgment on you who have let go out of anything but love. This
is meant to be a call to awareness for you.*

*When you let go with love, you release the energetic pattern of the situation,
and life can then shift into a new direction and vibration for you. When you let
go of a situation or a person, but still hold the anger, hatred, fear, or unfairness,
the energy of those feelings will draw to you the very situation or type of person
you just "let go of." This is not to punish you but to help you to see what is
within you, so that you may heal the wounds of anger, hatred, fear, etc.*

*How are you to heal those? Do not judge yourself for them but feel them.
Recognize that they are there…and then give them to me. It is not your place
to "get even," to make someone see their "wrong," for in doing so, you will keep
living and acting from your wounds. Your place is to heal the wounds that
have helped you to forget that you are a divine being of love and then bring
that love to your world.*

*When you see hatred in the world on your news—acts of violence—these are manifestations of a collective consciousness of what is in the individual hearts. Individual hearts create the collective heart. Look within to your own heart and see where you may bring healing to your smaller individual world. Once you have healed there, you then contribute to the healing of your global world. The time is now. You are killing yourselves and each other because of your own pain.*

*I am the light that helps you to feel love. And when you feel love, you are able to see it in your outside world. Feel it within first; see it outside of yourself. Feel; then see. Many do it backwards. They try to manifest something outside themselves in order to feel good within. It is a temporary "feel good" though.*

Yes, I've been there many times. I like this idea of feeling it first because I do know that we manifest what we feel, that the world outside of us reflects what is within us.

*So, if you don't like what you see…*

Look to what we feel…or were feeling…and bring healing to it?

*Yes, little one, you are remembering. The earth plane has a "time delay" because of the denseness of energy. And as you think and feel, the degree to which the timing of it manifests is related to the amount of resistance you hold, consciously or unconsciously.*

So, as I attempted to manifest a romantic relationship, the reason it was not transpiring was because I was resisting on some level?

*What did you learn at the "Creating Fulfilling Relationships" workshop this weekend?*

Well, when a couple of men I'd dated this past year stopped calling, I imagined they got scared of what they felt for me and ran. I'd get upset and think, "Ugh, another one who is not emotionally available…typical man!"

As I began to work with the feeling though, I realized that it stirred up in me a feeling that I wasn't special enough. That wound has festered within me for quite a bit of my life. I've seen where I've tried to overcompensate for it by looking for attention, etc. I realized that I dated from a place of neediness—needing someone to love me and make me feel special. And when they wouldn't or couldn't, they just touched upon the tender hurt that was already there. So as I bring healing to the wound, I am able to feel a greater love within me that I want to share from a healthier place.

*And as you bring awareness to wanting to share that love, little one, watch your life shift. You will attract a different type of man now, one who will reflect your willingness to share love.*

I am excited about it. And I want to help others do the same.

*And you will.*

Thank you.

God, can I get your input on something else? I was driving last week, and the thought came to me that I wanted to teach a workshop for people in recovery to offer healing for them. I'm sensing that underneath all these addictions, people desire the same thing: They want to feel your love.

*Very good.*

So, the title that I feel came from you was "From Recovery to Discovery." We keep re-covering up that wound, the ache, the void that can only be filled by your love. We cover it up repeatedly. Until we discover it and allow it to heal...

*And most use some substance or behavior that is not healthy...so before they are in recovery, they are in "wreckovery"—"wreck-over-y"—repeating the same "wreck" over and over again.*

I like that—it's so true. As I realized I wanted to do this program, I recognized I really needed it for myself to see the patterns that were not healthy in my own life.

*Sandy, many teach what they need to learn; it's beautiful. As you teach it, you'll integrate it more. Then you will move on to teach something else.*

Is there anything you want me to teach that I'm not getting?

*Little one, it matters not what you teach, for whatever you teach, you are teaching from love. Teach love. Help others to remember love. It need not be in a formal setting. As you show up as love, you show up as God. That, little one, is more than enough.*

Thank you, God, for this time; for this wisdom; for the people in my life who are on this journey with me; for my mom and sisters, my kids, my friends, and my clients. Help me to stay in love, so that it overflows to all that I come in contact with through my written and spoken word.

*And so it shall be.*

God, as I fixed my breakfast, I was reminded that this past summer when I would pray for a specific thing to happen and life responded differently, that that was the answer. But when it wasn't the response I wanted, I would sometimes say, "Oh yeah? You're not the boss of me!" like a little girl with her hands on her hips because she didn't get what she wanted! I'm so sorry, God. I'd have my little tantrum, just for a few minutes, maybe a half hour, or a couple of hours; I cried a little bit, picked myself back up, and moved on, realizing that sometimes unanswered prayers are a gift.

*Sandy, not only are they always gifts, but please understand that so many people stay in their tantrum for years upon years. You have helped many to break through; this book will help many more.*

So, when we don't know what to do here, God, because we *often* don't know, what should we do?

*Let it be okay that you don't have the answer in the moment. Life continually responds to your prayers. Watch what shows up at your door in terms of experience. And know that on some level, you needed the experience. How you move through it is up to you. Use your tools; use your heart. Your internal guidance system is there for you always.*

*October 14*

God, I sooo miss writing with you. It has been a busy six months; I've been in a new relationship since the beginning of May and learning about myself through it. We met by "accident" when I was at a restaurant with my son Austin and his friend, and he was there with a group of friends, one of whom I've known for twenty years.

When we were introduced, we both sensed a familiarity there but weren't sure where it originated. Later that night when I returned home, I realized where I had seen him before. I'd seen his profile on Match.com. We started emailing the next day and discovered a connective thread that we shared—loss.

His wife died from breast cancer at forty-four years old, almost two years ago. She and I share the same first name, which I think is interesting. And his boys, whom I have come to love, are about the same ages as Ariana and Austin. The six of us have a lot of fun together. He is very funny, handsome, generous, and successful. He is a beautiful person, God, and I am very grateful for his presence in my life. But we are so very different emotionally and spiritually.

*Sandy, you are matched to help bring out the best in each other.*

That's good to know because it doesn't always feel like that. He's unlike any other man I've been with. We don't talk about you, God, or about Spirit or spirituality. To him, prayer is a private thing, and he has no desire to understand or to know about Spirit.

*Sandy, sometimes, in order to bring out the best in someone, the other issues have to be addressed first.*

Like the insecurities that came up for me a few times? There have been many moments where I just wanted to hear sweet, tender words, but they weren't there. Those moments made me feel needy and at times empty, and he didn't fill that space inside me.

*Nor was it his job to. You have used the tools to surrender the sadness and re-fill yourself with my love.*

Yes, I have. I find that it is the only thing that can fill me when I stumble into those moments.

*Then do it as often as you need to.*

Thank you for the reminder. God, I would like some guidance about my work. I want to write more. The creative process of writing feeds my soul. I love how it feels to say, "I'm a writer." I sometimes envision myself as a full-time writer…spending time writing by a lake (I've never actually done that) in the peace I am in love with. I don't always need to know where my writing is going, but I enjoy putting the pieces together and seeing the end result.

*Sandy, you are in the moment when you write, right?*

Yes.

*Notice other times and places you have been truly happy because you were in the moment. Don't discount that; it counts for a lot. So you want to see yourself writing more and call yourself a writer/author. You already are. So call yourself that; see how it feels. Whatever you would like to be…or see yourself as…claim it, call yourself that, and you will become it. Many of you have practiced that already but in a negative way. For instance, thoughts of "I never have enough money; I can't seem to find anyone worth dating, and I don't have enough time" are not positive ideas. Bring awareness to your words because they are not very becoming, but they are becoming who you are.*

Nice play on words, God.

*Step into what you want. By taking the time to write this morning, you move into the vibration of writer…remembering what it feels like.*

That's so true. And I'll admit that I love to write in a pair of sweatpants and sweatshirt or in my pajamas and big, pink, fuzzy slippers. It really doesn't matter what I look like when I write; it's the process that works.

*Sandy, many will be able to identify with what they want to be but will continue to focus on why it is not present in their lives. They will continue to keep it at bay, or at the very least, slow down the process of what they want coming into their lives.*

I'm hearing that song, "If you want it, here it is, come and get it..."

*That's only partly true. I'd rather shift it to "If you want it...here it is... be open to receive it." Open your heart. Know that it is already yours.*

Let me try this thought: I can feel a million dollars.

*Good, if that is what you truly want, it is yours.*

I ask that it'll come in a healthy, positive way for the highest and greatest good of all. I'd take a year or two off and write and write and write. Actually, I don't need a million. I could do that with $100,000.

*But if you received that money, would you really trust and take that time off? Or would you invest it for the future with the fear that you'd need it later and then continue working?*

You're reading my mind, aren't you? I just thought, "I could keep my practice open part time and invest part of that money...just in case after those one to two years are done I didn't bring in any income from the writing," which is silly.

*So cancel the thought. And trust that it may come to you in a way that you are not envisioning. Be open to how it will come to you.*

Done! I envision being supported by the universe with enough money to take one year off to truly focus on my writing. So, $100,000 comes to me easily. (I can feel my resistance to this.)

*Where does the conflict stem from?*

From what others would think. What would my ex-husband think? I imagine that he'd think it would be irresponsible.

*And you are going to let that stop you and what you know your soul has been nudging you to do? Sandy, you are too strong for that, and you know it.*

I am. Thank you. This is truly exciting. I have no idea how the $100,000 is going to manifest. But I trust that it will. Wow, this is a different concept that I hadn't even thought of. I will be able to focus on freelance articles, to finish this book and another I'm working on and to publish *The Little Seed of Hope* book.

I love being a writer, and people love to read what I write. I receive compliments on it all the time! Oh, I am extremely excited. I let this be; I open my heart and soul for this experience in the highest and greatest manifestation for all involved. Thank you, God.

*It was your idea, little one. I just reminded you that it was possible.*

*October 16*

So, God, what would you like to talk about today?

*What's on your mind, Sandy?*

Well, I'm thinking about how I love having a day off—to get the house in order, to go food shopping, to start cooking for our dinner party on Saturday night. Alright, that sounds somewhat boring. Let me think a little more. Okay, I feel a little heaviness in my chest from my conversation last night with my boyfriend about his son and the challenge with his grades in school.

*What is your concern?*

My concern is that he will come down too hard on his son and not hear him out entirely, and his son would withdraw, not wanting to share what he's feeling.

*Sandy, your friend grew up with a different set of parenting conditions than you.*

I know; so is there anything I can say to him that will help him with his son?

*Dearest one, please tell him to hold no worry around the future of his son. His son is here as a teacher of sorts. In his own way, he creates his path and in the process pushes some of his father's fear buttons. His father then begins to* question, *"What if he stops trying and applying himself altogether…what will he end up like?"* *Please tell your friend to hold no energy there. Tell him to look within himself to see where his self-expectations came up short. Tell him he could not have saved his wife. He could not fix her. She had a journey of her own to follow. His job is to bring all aspects of himself back to love.*

God, he won't understand this at all. I can't share it with him.

*So speak it to his heart and soul in your meditation.*

That I can do. Thank you, God. Sometimes I grow frustrated when I don't know the right words to say that will help someone move out of their pain.

*Sandy, it is not always up to you. This is one of the lessons that you are in the midst of—not taking responsibility for others' pain, happiness, and satisfaction. Those emotions are up to the individual and are not within your control.*
*As far as your friend not embracing your gift as a medium, allow him to be where he is. You cannot force an understanding on him. He loves you; he just cannot wrap his mind around the concept of Spirit.*

I know, but it hurts when he won't engage in a discussion about it. I even connected with his wife in Spirit for him a few months ago but that still didn't convince him. God, my clients are so very grateful when I connect with their loved ones in Spirit for them. It's just odd—to have this man, who is my partner right now, not believe in it.

Actually, as I sit with this, I am reminded that he did tell me that after his wife died, he greatly wanted her to send him a sign, and he waited for six months and received no sign. Then he gave up hope. So, when I started sensing her around me, he agreed to sit and allow me to bring through her spirit energy for him. It was challenging because I already knew his story, her story, their children, etc., but it was still an honor. But it held little meaning for him, and that hurt. I guess he had a different expectation of what it would be like.

*Sandy, there were expectations on both parts. He expected you to provide one specific detail that you were not able to, and you assumed he would embrace your gift the way you have it.*

Some people do come in for a reading and expect that I'll be able to give them the nickname that their grandfather had for them when they were twelve years old. It doesn't really work that way. At times, I am frustrated when I can't meet someone's expectations.

*It's all about expectations and wanting to be loved and appreciated. Think about this. Do you worry or hold any concern about what I expect from you?*

I've never thought about that. No, I don't worry about that because I know you love me unconditionally and recognize that you don't hold expectations…only love.

*Sandy, stop for a moment and let that sink in. I don't hold expectations… only love. How would that shift every part of your life if you really believed and lived that? There are no expectations on you, other than the ones you agree to take on yourself. I don't hold expectations…only love.*

Wait. I have to take a minute with this. What's flooding into my mind is this…God is love. God doesn't expect anything of me. God just is…love. God loves and asks nothing in return. So, here I've been trying to please other people, and I've exhausted myself in the process…for what? To be accepted? To be loved? I already am—by God, unconditionally. Wow. This is enough for today. I've been loving out of order.

*Sandy, what would happen if you didn't please everybody or even anybody?*

I'd still be loved. I'd still have love. But my fear tells me that their love is more important because I probably wasn't remembering how loved I already am. Oh, my mind is going to explode. I don't know how I can verbalize this; I think I just need to be with it and let it sink in—let it integrate. It is such a simple concept, but one that is very hard to fathom because it is so simple. We have complicated this whole idea of love by trying to gain approval from others when we had it all along…from God. I think I have to go meditate on this. I'll be back, God. What a gift you gave me. Thank you.

*November 15*

God, I'm still trying to integrate that last lesson about love because I keep allowing myself to feel the emptiness when I don't feel loved in the way I'm used to being loved. There's a part of me that knows better, but I become caught up in a moment sometimes and sense a void right in the center of my being.

I recently woke up in the middle of the night, feeling so sad and empty, and I told you, "Okay, God, this has to be about me and you!" I'm sensing, as I told a friend yesterday, that perhaps it is my soul's journey at this time to truly stay connected to you. Because when I am, I have peace.

It's as if I'm being asked to grow up, and I sometimes fight it, having a little inner tantrum. When I connect with you, God, there is such peace. You don't have to say anything. You just are love, and I envelop myself in it. There is nothing better than that. It fills me completely.

*But you still expect your friend to love you differently, Sandy.*

Yes, and I keep getting stuck there. Can you help me to see it from a different perspective?

*You keep approaching the "wrong well" to fill you. It's as simple as that. He does love you…a lot by the way. You are a different bird to him. He does not recognize your language yet. But he loves you. He shows his love differently.*

He does. And I've told him what makes me feel most loved—romantic words and so on—but I'm not sure he understands me.

*Look at that word "understand." He doesn't "under stand" you or rather "stand under" you because you are standing on your own two feet. Do you understand?*

This is becoming funny. Yes, God, I do understand how important it is for me to fill any void with you. Please help me to heal the resistance to that—the thoughts that tell me that human love is more important than your love.

*Sandy, there is only one love, for my love is the source of all love. Some allow it in a little bit; some allow it in more. The degree to which they permit it in and let the flow be expressed through them has to do with them. Human love, as you put it, is my love, but it has been filtered.*

*Your friend is doing the best he possibly can with the filters he has in place—as are you. You become aware of old insecurity when you don't feel emotionally connected in your relationship. A lack of verbal affection and praise triggers this insecurity. Then you feel sad, and then you turn to me and remember what your source is, and then you feel peace once again. Do you see that all roads lead to home?*

Yes, I do. I will always find my way back to you. Sometimes I take the short route; sometimes I take a detour.

*Sandy, when you connect with me, do I shower you with words of praise and affection?*

No. It is a feeling…rather, a knowing, a remembering. "Aaah" is how I would describe it.

*And do you have any expectations of me?*

No, because you are love. Simply put.

*So, understand this…stand under this. Fill yourself with my love continually. You'll see how your life shifts. I promise you, it will.*

Thank you, God.

God, do you have any advice for the program I'm doing tomorrow night? It's the biggest audience I've ever had for the "Messages from Heaven" program; it's to be held in a high school auditorium. I'm more excited than nervous.

*That is a good sign because you are coming from a higher place…of love. Fill yourself during the day tomorrow; you will be giving a lot of energy to them. Tell them I said hello and tell them that I am here for them. Remind them that pain is optional. Sadness is temporary. My love is continual.*

God, why is loss so hard for us here? I'm not sure we covered that in previous conversations. Sometimes I just cry for others' pain, knowing the ache of loss is unbearable at times for them.

*Sandy, please hear this. The pain is a signal that there is a disconnect. When they remember their connection to me, there is no pain.*

But why would people choose not to remember and stay in pain?

*Sometimes because they don't think it's possible to not hurt or they believe they **should** be in pain because they have "lost" someone physically. More often, they have thought (as you have) that human love is more important than divine love. Loving out of order.*

But how can I say to people, "Just turn to God and feel God's love… and you won't feel pain."

*You have been saying it. Some have listened; some weren't ready to give up the pain. Dearest little one, when each of you came to this earth plane, you were created as physical form with my spirit within you at the same time. So, I am always with you; you know that wisdom in the depths of your being. Many don't pay attention to my spirit essence within them as they focus more on the physical. But the corporeal is only temporary. When the bodily form dies, the spirit continues.*

So why are we all so attached to the physical here? It hurts so much when the bodily form of someone we love is no longer here. We've adopted strong messages from society that the physical aspect of who we are is more important.

*Do you sense that shifting towards more spiritual awareness?*

Yes, it is. But letting go of the physical form is a struggle for so many. It had been for me and still can be at times.

*Sandy, your soul chose to take on a heavy journey of loss and challenge, so that you could experience what it is like to re-remember and then help others to recall the truth. In other lifetimes, you stayed in darkness throughout and were blind to the truth. In this lifetime, you are a messenger for many. We are happy that you have chosen to wake up. You are going through "growing pains" with your new lessons of external expression of another's love as compared to internal affirmation of my love. You try so hard to integrate it within your being. Drop the idea that it has to be difficult. This relationship is perfect to help you with this lesson. You called it forth for that reason. Little one, affirm, "I am in God's love, and that is enough for me."*

I love that... it is a deep truth for me. When I am in God's love, I truly don't need anything from anyone else and what I do receive is a blessing. I love that it is so simple. Thank you, thank you, thank you! I'm going to go meditate with it. Thank you, God. "I am in God's love, and that is enough for me. I am in God's love, and that is enough for me. I am in God's love, and that is enough for me." I feel like I am Dorothy in the Wizard of Oz, clicking my heels three times and saying, "There's no place like home; there's no place like home; there's no place like home."

*You are beginning to see that "home"…is my love. Dorothy was right—there's no place like home.*

*November 23*

Hi, God, why is it that whenever I reread what we've written together, it brings me to a place of peace? No matter what I'm feeling, no matter what is going on in my life, your words provide comfort and peace.

*And this surprises you because…*

Ha ha…sometimes you seem so human to me.

*Sometimes you seem so human to me too, and I say that with love.*

I imagine it also surprises me because of how simple it is. Your words bring a feeling of comfort and peace.

*The words don't bring comfort and peace, Sandy: They **are** the vibration of comfort and peace, you choose to draw them to yourself.*

When I connect with your energy in meditation, I feel a powerful vibration, a "buzzing" within me. In those moments, I experience you as the vibration of love. Is it ever possible for us to remember you, to feel your presence all the time? I don't, and in my moments of not remembering, I feel insecure and fearful. Almost like one of those old, Fisher Price "Close and Play" record players: close it, it plays; open it, it stops. "Remember God, there's peace. Forget God, there's everything else."

*Sandy, you chose this journey to remember the essence of those words through all different kinds of experiences. You move through the lessons well.*

*At times, you tend to judge yourself when you forget. Please don't do that. It matters not how many times you forget but that you are willing to remember once more again. I don't need you to remember for me; it is not for my benefit. You do it for yourself. Let me say that again, for some religions have diluted the message. I don't need you to remember me for me; you do it for yourself.*

*It draws you to the peace I placed within you from the beginning of all time. Many of you have searched all your lives for what brings you to peace. It is already within you. It has been within you all along—through every workshop you have attended, through every self-help book you have read. You have played a cosmic game of hide and seek—hiding your true essence from yourself…seeking outside yourself to find it, feeling frustration and despair, wanting to give up, then finally remembering to look inward, where your true essence has been all along.*

*Many of you refer to this as experiencing heaven on earth. Remember in one of our prior conversations that heaven is not a place but a consciousness of love. So how would you experience heaven (love) on earth? Move the "h" in "earth" to the beginning of the word, to make it "heart." You experience heaven on earth by living from your heart. Heaven…is in your heart.*

*January 6*

Good morning, God. Happy New Year to you! Has anyone ever wished you a happy New Year?

*Well, there really is no division of time in this realm, so it's rather a "happy new moment." That is all there is anyway.*

God, I've noticed lately how frequently my thoughts are not in the present moment. Ugh.

*Where are they?*

My thoughts? Well, sometimes I find myself wondering what my future will be.

*Wondering, Sandy, or worrying?*

You got me, yes, worrying…

(*Note from Sandy: I'm not sure where I went after that…I probably became distracted or went to find a snack!*)

*January 21*

God, I still struggle at times with this relationship I'm in. I feel like I need to look at it differently because the same issues keep recurring. So I imagine I'm not learning some part of the lesson.

I do have peace when I practice Byron Katie's work—by looking at my thoughts. I usually see some deeper truth about myself. I know on some level that it is not about me trying to change anyone. Why do I keep becoming entangled here?

*Dear little one, you allow your fear to rest in your awareness—fear of "does he not love me enough? Will it get easier? Is he the right one for me?" The answers (in order) are...yes, he loves you enough, it is what it is, and he is the right one for you, in this moment.*

God, the pain that arises in my heart feels so real. I'm mourning for something that I want but don't possess. In doing so, I find it hard to appreciate what I have with him that is beautiful.

*What do you still have with him?*

Moments...shared moments, sometimes alone...sometimes not.

*Let it all be, Sandy. There is much that you cannot possibly see in this moment. It will all play out perfectly, and let me tell you, there is no other place for you to be but where you are, moving through this all. Please do not judge yourself for journeying through it. Your relationship culls to the surface a deep belief that you have held in this lifetime.*

That's what it feels like—and right now, my chest feels so heavy.

*Breathe, little one, breathe. The heaviness is the pressure you put on yourself to know the answers right now, to figure it all out immediately. Relax, little one. I am here.*

Thank you, God. So, this belief that I've held in this lifetime that is coming to the surface…what is it?

*It is a learning from your soul, which you set up to move through in this lifetime. It may be resolved in this relationship, but it doesn't have to be. Do the best you can. Would you like to know the belief that you've held, the one that has challenged you all your life that is ready to be challenged?*

Yes, please.

*It is **"I need to feel loved."***

Oh, God…

*Notice I did not say "I need to **be** loved." My words were "I need to **feel** loved."*

There's so much history in those five words, so much invested in them, trying to prove that it is true. I've spent so much energy there. But what do you mean challenge the belief?

*See if that thought is true for you. Do you really need to feel loved?*

Well, yes, of course! We all do. Don't we?

*Many people believe that and live their lives expecting others to feed that need. If you let truth shine on this thought, it will unravel, and you will be free of the energy that keeps you stuck. So, let's work with it, shall we?*

Absolutely.

*Do you know you are loved?*

From you, yes. From others, I guess I've vacillated between believing it and not believing due to their behavior and their words.

*How do you know you are loved by me?*

Because that is what you are. You are love. You just love.

*But you don't always feel it.*

Right.

*So, does that mean that I don't always love you because you don't always feel it?*

No, your love is still there.

*And if you imagine my love is pure, do you see the misled belief that others, who struggle themselves, should always be able to show their love?*

Yes, I do, but I'm missing something here.

*You are loved.*

Yes.

*But you don't always feel it when you look to another human to give love to you.*

Absolutely true.

*So, you place another's love as more important than Source love.*

Why do I still do that? It's *insane!*

*Yes, little one, it is. Many of you play out insanity, and whenever you tire of it, you'll come out of it. It is not to be judged though. So, now look at "I need to feel loved." How have you asked others to support that thought?*

I'm feeling naked here. And I'm resisting sharing this, because my readers will know I'm not perfect.

*And that's why they love you, Sandy. They see themselves through your words.*

Okay. I'll share. I think I've expected that a man should love me in a certain way because I needed to feel loved. I've looked for approval from… just about everyone because I needed to feel loved. I've waited for my kids' appreciation because I needed to feel loved. I've tried to please others because I needed to feel loved.

*When a man, or your kids, or the world shows you love, appreciates you, or approves of you, what happens?*

I feel very peaceful in my heart.

*And when this man, or your kids, or the world didn't show you love, appreciate you, or approve of you, what happened?*

Well, I typically felt like they didn't care or that somehow I wasn't enough.

*Good, Sandy, you're seeing the fear for what it is. Sandy, what happens on a given day when you remember to connect to me through prayer or through this dialog?*

I feel very peaceful, again, in my heart.

*Yes. Now follow the thread of fear attached to the thought of "I need to feel loved." What would happen if you didn't feel it?*

My fear would be if I didn't feel loved, then I'd feel alone...and lonely...and very sad.

*So what would happen if you were very sad?*

I'd cry; then I imagine I'd turn to you, release my sadness, and remember that you are always there.

*And then what?*

Then I'd experience peace again.

*So, do you really need to feel loved?*

Wow, I guess I don't. I believed in that thought—I invested in it so heavily. I really don't need to feel loved in order to be peaceful?

*You just said it. See how it feels when you say that statement.*

I really don't need to feel loved in order to be okay. Oh my God, it is so peaceful. I don't need to feel loved, because deep in my heart, I know I AM loved.

*Sandy, you can play out the whole scenario whichever way you choose. You can allow the fear to manifest, feel alone, feel very sad, and then turn to me and release it and remember that I am always there and then be in peace or you can connect with me first, remember that I am always there, and be in peace without having to bring forth all the fear.*

God, is it that simple?

*It is.*

Am I missing something here, though? Honestly…is there something else I'm missing? And how come others don't have to go through all of this?

*Sandy, you are not missing anything—except peace. Not all will go through the same lesson because it may not be in their soul contract. It is in yours. And you are willing to feel it all. Not all people are. Some numb themselves to the pain and/or stress in their lives. And they may not reach the peace that underlies it. So they may live their life…under lies.*

So, this is not about my relationship with this man?

*Little one, it is not. The remembrance of peace and love can come through relationships, through work, through children. You have chosen to move through it through relationships. And are you ready for this?*

What?

*There is nothing wrong with you.*

Are you just saying that because you want me to feel better?

*Would I do that?*

No.

*There is nothing wrong with you.*

And I don't need to feel loved?

*No.*

Wow, what would I do with the energy that I expended all my life, trying to feel loved? I've played out this story in so many ways. Thank you, God. I sense there's a lot more to this. I don't need to feel loved. I don't need to feel loved. It is freeing.

*Perhaps you would take that energy that you used trying to **feel** loved and use it to simply love others.*

This is larger than I can realize. Thank you. Please help me to remember this truth, to integrate it, to live in it, and to share it with others. I sense I need to be with it first for a while, to try it on, to relish in the energy of it.

*Let it be. Let yourself bask in the freedom of it. It is yours.*

I also recognize that no one could've taught me this. It is not a new concept. But for some reason, I'm willing to hear it now. I had to go through the pain and sadness of the illusion coming undone, in order to cultivate it from within. This man in my life, without even knowing it, helped me to reach the gift of this awareness.

*Dearest little one, illusions cannot stand up to the truth. The walls had to tumble down; the pain you experienced felt real. It represented the walls toppling over to show vulnerability, so that you may understand the truth that waited for you all along. Welcome home.*

Home, to me, feels like my truth.

*It is, little one. Welcome home.*

*January 22*

Good morning, God. Much more peace has dwelled in my heart since yesterday's conversation with you. I can't believe I bought into that belief for so long. Understanding the untruth of the sponsoring thought of "I need to *feel* loved" has helped me return to a softer place within myself.

And I don't feel like I need to run around shouting, "Look at the truth I've found! Look at the truth I've found!" I've done that before when I've gotten excited about a new diet that I'd try for a day and told my family and friends, "*This* is going to be the one to help me lose those last ten pounds!" Then I've stopped following it two days later!

*Dearest little one, this awareness doesn't need to be shouted—simply lived.*

I felt it last night with my clients. I showed up differently—with a quiet inner peace and a softness to my voice. I loved how I presented myself, and Spirit worked with me much more easily from my perspective. There was no mind chatter of "I hope this makes sense. I hope I connect with who they want me to connect with. I hope this is good enough." I didn't feel any of that. I felt peace, and it was a great night.

*Welcome home, little one.*

God, I also noticed this morning that I experienced no heaviness from the thoughts that would normally greet me upon awakening. They usually arrive with a slight uneasiness in my chest. How did I let that be the norm for so long?

*Sandy, it was part of how you played this lesson out. Let yourself be with it all. You don't need to cling to any concern as to how long you'll be able to hold this feeling. Just be in it with no fear around it.*

God, I keep thinking of all that I've done, the ways I've acted, and the things I've said to support that thought of "I need to feel loved." I'm awaking from a dream.

*Or rather, awaking from a nightmare?*

Ha ha…yes, that is more like it because more often than not, it was not peaceful. No matter how much I had in my life, it was never enough. No one and no thing could have ever been enough. Oh my God, such peace exists in this awareness.

*Yes, it does, dear one. Live it. Love it. As you integrate it more, you'll be able to share it with others who are ready.*

I don't feel I have the words to share it yet—not in a way that would make sense to people. I am free, God. It is what I have wanted to feel all my life: to be free from this pattern. Thank you. Oddly, I just ordered Byron Katie's book, *I Need Your Love…Is That True?* It hasn't arrived yet, but I feel I've already assimilated the book's entirety in the gift you presented me yesterday.

*Sandy, that is how manifestation works in Spirit. You are beginning to see that and, more importantly, experience it. Spirit holds a thought, and it becomes instantaneously real for them.*

This is awesome!

*Play with it. Stay centered in your truth. Do it all with love.*

I want to be aware of the pattern I've played out—all the ways that I've repeated the story of "I need to feel loved." Can you help me? Where do I even start?

*Look to how you've held unhappiness because you thought your need to feel loved could be filled outside of you. Start when you were a young child…*

I remember feeling sad as a little girl in elementary school, playing on the playground, feeling like I didn't fit in with the other kids. I was chubby, and I was the smartest one in my class (a wonderful combo). That need to feel loved caused me to learn how to be a people pleaser, especially with teachers. So the teachers all loved me because I was a model student, never getting in trouble. As I grew older, I hung out with my sisters and cousins, but I didn't have many friends. I didn't drink or smoke, and I wasn't invited to the popular parties, so at school, I often felt like an outsider looking in. I wish I'd known you then, God.

*I was there, but you went through life the way you were meant to. How about with your family?*

I belong to the greatest family. I'm the youngest of five girls, and we're all very close still. But I do remember feeling jealous of my sisters when I was younger; I thought I could never be as pretty as Cindy, as musically talented as Nancy, or as funny as Penny. And all the boys liked Susie, who was only two years older than me. I felt like I couldn't measure up to them. The need to feel loved showed up as wanting attention, which may have fueled a desire to succeed in life...as an overachiever. I understand now that it was all in my mind, the way I chose to see myself back then. I didn't know how to do it differently though.

*No, you didn't, little one. How did it show up in your marriage or in other relationships?*

Well, I longed for a deeper emotional and spiritual connectedness in my marriage and didn't find it. That need to feel loved was extremely strong, and I felt empty often and thought it was because of him. I realize now, that it wasn't. There was a void that back then I thought my husband should have filled.

With other relationships, I don't know if I'd ever felt whole, so I imagine that I looked to the other person to make me whole. I'm not sure it's anyone's responsibility to do that for another. So with dating, that need to feel loved appeared as not setting healthier boundaries...saying yes, even though my inner sense said no. Needing to hear that I was sexy or that I was beautiful—that made me feel loved. Always smiling, a façade I lived with for years because I so longed to be liked or loved. "Aren't you so nice?" Smile, yes, I am. Now I know I am lovable...from the inside out.

Looking back now, I can see that I attempted to "get" people to love me, probably because I didn't really love myself. These experiences have taught me that it's alright to say no and risk disappointing another, so as not to disappoint myself.

*Good insight, Sandy. How about with your children?*

With Ari and Austin, I remember when Ari was an infant, maybe four or five weeks old. I spent my every moment caring for her, and I distinctly remember one sleepless night changing her diaper, exhausted and in tears because I felt no appreciation for all that I did for her. Oh, God, that's so weird. She was an infant! But that thought was there. With Austin, he had so many tantrums as a little child—what a little bugger. I probably gave in to him more quickly than I should have because I wanted him to be happy. And as my kids grew, the need to feel loved throbbed as a deep longing to feel appreciated in return for all that I did for them, and I sometimes experienced a little resentment when I didn't receive it.

After my divorce, the need to feel loved manifested as a fear of my former husband providing more "stuff" for my kids. "What if they love him more? What if they want to go live with him?" You helped me through that fear. Thank you.

*You're doing well, Sandy; these moments of complete honesty allow you to be vulnerable and transparent for your readers. They will see themselves in you. What about with your work?*

I love the way I'm able to help my clients; I love the workshops that I teach. My need to feel loved has shown up there too though. It's manifested when I compare myself to other mediums, authors, or healers and worry that I'm not as good or that I should've progressed further in reaching larger audiences or sold-out crowds because others are. I realize, God, that I only experience fear when I'm not fully aware of your presence in my heart.

As I look at what I've just written, I can see that it was all part of what I had to go through in this lifetime for the sake of my own growth. Thank you, God, for the gift of awareness. I don't need to feel loved. I am loved. I am love. I don't need to feel loved. I forgive myself for not knowing how to go through life differently, and I am grateful that now I know. I feel like I've been reborn.

*Sandy, it is what you prayed for, isn't it?*

Yes, and these truths have set me free. I'm in a new life with new opportunities. Who I was is no longer. I have stepped out of that shell. I will enjoy seeing what life brings now and how my outer world will alter because of this inner shift. I don't need to feel loved. I truly don't know what my future holds, and it is all okay. I trust that I will attract the perfect experiences for me. This man now in my life showed up for me and unknowingly helped me to get to this moment. And thank you, God. I couldn't have done this without you.

*Most welcome, little one. Remember I am always here with you.*

God, I drove to the grocery store this morning and found myself smiling, for no reason! I smiled, not because anyone had done or said something to make me smile but simply because I wanted to smile. It was like my heart was smiling.

I don't know if I have the words to explain this shift yet. I bumped into an old friend at Stop & Shop this morning and tried explaining this change. His comment was, "But of course you need to feel loved—we all do." I didn't know how to respond, especially in the cake mix aisle of the supermarket. I'm not certain how to describe what I'm feeling or how I arrived here in terms that others will understand.

*But that is okay. It is an unspeakable joy. Let it be. Let it grow. Let it move you into new moments of grace. All is well. And if you forget again, I will remind you once again—with love.*

God, how could I ever forget this? It is too powerful to me.

*I hear you. But if you do happen to forget, I'll be right there with you to lovingly remind you one more time.*

*January 23*

God, I still find myself smiling more and waking up feeling free. It's as if you've endured the hiccups for a long time and now they've gone away. You wait to see if they're really, really gone. When you realize that they are, it's a great feeling!

I noticed some interesting things lately. My appetite and eating habits are shifting. I'm making healthier choices, not eating until I'm stuffed and not snacking when I'm not hungry. I shared that with a friend today at the gym (yes, I went back after not going for about a month!), and I heard myself saying to her, "I think I was hungering for love." I wonder if I expected others to feed that need to feel loved and they couldn't. Maybe I tried to feed it in a different way with food? Is there a connection?

*What do you know in your heart?*

That maybe I'd always hungered for something that no one could ever give me. So I used food.

*That is correct, little one. Let your body do what it does; it will let you know when it is hungry and when it is full. It will let you know when it is thirsty or tired or in pain. Let your body guide you to what it needs.*

Thank you. God, I'm also beginning to understand with this awareness—how I struggled for so long with the idea of not having expectations! People would say to me, "Sandy, stop expecting your boyfriend to be different. He is who he is." And I knew that, but I realize now that

I couldn't release those expectations because the thought of "I need to feel loved" had to be addressed. I see it so clearly now. The expectations led to frustration, which led to looking at the thought, which led to truth, which leads to peace. I had to reach the sponsoring thought, in order to have peace, right?

*It seems to make sense to you. Keep going.*

I don't need anyone to be different for me. I can be present in the moment with love and compassion. I have found that even my boyfriend seems a little different. Maybe he feels no pressure from me now. What a turnaround from the way things were.

No wonder I've been so tired. I presume that all that anxiety held a low vibration of energy. I am so grateful, God, that I was ready for this awareness. Help me to live this peace in every moment of now.

*You don't need to worry, dear one, for it is truly who you are—in your very essence.*

I can just breathe and rest, and let life unfold. Thank you, thank you, thank you!

So, God, I discerned something interesting today with a couple of clients. One seemed to be struggling so much in her life. So, I helped her find the sponsoring thought that was behind all her pain.

*And what was it?*

It was "I should be different than who I am." She said that thought has fueled most of her unpleasant experiences where she fights against herself. It was like watching a light being illuminated within her. I pray she continues to work with it.

*So, did she come up with that or did you, Sandy?*

Um...ugh...well, she came up with a few of the first little fearful thoughts, but it was you, or was it me, who deciphered the sponsoring thought?

*We are one. I whispered it to **her** at the same time, but you heard it first. In your excitement, little one, you so desire for people to "get it." Let your clients hear my voice; they've been asking how to do it. Hold the space for them.*

I understand. I will hold the space for them. And my second client, whose dad died just three weeks ago, was in such pain. She wanted to feel peace again but couldn't. So I helped her to find her painful sponsoring thought. I heard it first again—sorry. It was "Death is a bad thing." She discovered that she has lived most of her life trying to keep death away, avoiding the idea of death, exhausting herself, while trying to protect everyone around her because her belief was—death is a bad thing. We worked with the thought, and she realized that perhaps it wasn't even true. She can understand it now. She found the reasons herself.

She said, "Death is not a bad thing because my dad no longer has cancer and is no longer suffering…Death is not a bad thing because it is a new beginning…Death is not a bad thing because it is freeing for the person who has died."

*Good, very good.*

Wait, there was more. When she held the thought, "Death is a bad thing," knowing that her dad just died, she said it kept her from accepting reality and made her anxious. When she turned it around to "death is not a bad thing," she said her energy felt lighter. I believe that whenever we shift a low vibration thought to a higher energy thought, our outer lives change in a wonderful way. So, do we all have different sponsoring thoughts that we have carried around for most of the lives that are part of our soul contract?

*Yes, but most are different variations that lead back to the same central theme, "I am separate from God." All thoughts, if followed past fear, will lead to home…to peace.*

And, God, another funny thing happened today. Remember this idea of manifesting thought more quickly? This afternoon, I glanced at my living room hardwood floors, thinking, "I really need to wash these floors." About ten seconds later, Ariana went to grab a drink from the refrigerator and cans of Diet Coke started free-falling from the top of the refrigerator. SPLAT—all of them fell on the floor. Two of them exploded all over the kitchen and living room floors. Ariana, now drenched in Diet Coke, screamed, not knowing what to do! I couldn't help but smile and giggle. It gave me the opportunity to clean the darn floors. Talk about manifesting a wish quickly!

*January 24*

Good morning, God. Can we talk about the body and weight issues? I want to bounce some things off you to see if they stand true.

*Good morning to you, little one. How are you feeling?*

I'm still feeling very free and happy. And I feel lighter in the way I'm relating to Ariana, Austin, and in my relationship. No pressure, just experiencing light conversations and more laughter—it feels good.

*Good for you. So, what would you like to discuss?*

This whole idea of weight loss, what the weight represents, and what feeds excess weight as it relates to these sponsoring thoughts.

*Go on.*

I realized yesterday I expected people to feed this need to feel loved. Sometimes they could, but it wasn't their job. And as I think back, I realize that when they did feed this need, I tended to eat less because I felt filled inside.

But when they didn't feed this need, I ate more because there was a void that wanted to be filled. But it didn't need food—it needed love and understanding. It needed an awareness of you. God, what desires are within us that we look to the outside world to fill? What do people truly hunger for?

*It may be physical love, approval, acceptance, appreciation, understanding, trust, peace...shall I go on? It can be summed up in one word—love—an awareness that they are not separate from me. That hunger may be filled by the outside world, but it is usually temporary. My love and peace are already within. Once you remember that, you will see its reflection in others around you.*

Can we apply this to finances? The hunger for more money?

*Sure, let's start with you.*

But I don't have an issue with money. Although, I do sometimes worry that I don't have much set aside for retirement.

*So, what is the thought, Sandy?*

I don't have enough saved for me to retire.

*So you should save more for retirement? How do you know you will reach retirement?*

What are you trying to say?

*That it would be best for you to release the worry.*

Because I'm going to die before retirement age?

*I'm not saying that. But look at the peace you have in your life in this moment. It is so different from one year ago or even one week ago, right?*

Absolutely!

*Last week, you didn't know this peace. Now you do. So don't project fear or worry into the future based on what you have in the bank right now. Anything can and will happen, Sandy. Free yourself, and let life unfold. You will always have more than enough. Do you trust that? There are other sources of financial flow than what's in your bank account in this moment.*

I do believe that.

*Release the worry by challenging the thought.*

So, what I have now is perfect for right now.

*How does that feel?*

Peaceful.

But what about the future? Will it be enough for the future?

*Little one, you are funny today. What can you remember about the future that feels the most peaceful to you?*

That the future really doesn't exist. This moment of now is all I have, and I can choose to feel calmness in it. When I feel peaceful right now, I attract the next perfect thing, which will show me the way that life unfolds perfectly.

*Amen.*

Amen. Thanks, God; you're the best.

*You are of the same fabric—cut of the same cloth.*

Thank you. God, more is unraveling about how my thoughts can ensnare me in stress! I drove to the bank this morning and thought about how many times I have nagged my kids to clean their rooms. They would, but then a day or so later, their rooms would be back to what they were comfortable with.

It occurred to me today—they don't want what I want. I long for their rooms to be clean. They don't share the same view. So, I'd tried to overpower what they wanted; after all, I'm the Mom! Why do I need their rooms to be clean? Because…their rooms are supposed to be clean! Plus, it feels so good for me to have my room clean! I laugh as I write this because I can finally see it clearly. I want their rooms to be clean because I love how it feels when my room is clean. If it were equally important to them, they'd clean their rooms!

I don't have to badger them to take a shower because they value a clean body (thank you, God!). I couldn't stop laughing to myself at how silly these thoughts seemed all of a sudden. Here I was trying to impose on them how good I feel when my room is clean. Maybe they enjoy having it the way it is. And if I didn't spend so much time and energy reminding them again and again, I'd be a more loving and playful mom.

So I told them this afternoon with love in my heart and a smile on my face, "I am no longer going to require you guys to keep your rooms clean. If you value a clean room, then you'll clean it. Otherwise, keep the door shut."

I have placed so many judgments on clean and what I imagine "messy" to mean about a person. Austin looked surprised and happy as if he wasn't sure he could trust this alien mom who was speaking to him.

Ariana said, "Mom, will you please remind me to clean it though?"

I smiled and hugged her, "No, honey, I won't. It's up to you. If it's what you want, you'll do it." I can breathe easier, and I feel peace! I love this. I wonder what other shoulds/judgments will unravel, and I can only imagine that it will bring even more peace, but I don't know that to be true. I love how I feel right now.

*March 21*

Hi, God, it's been a while, though I know you've been with me.

*How do you know, Sandy?*

Because I know that that is the nature of who/what you are.

*Good. Now, do you know the nature of who/what YOU are?*

We're starting pretty quickly this morning, no chit chat?

*Would you rather I start with a joke?*

No, I'm good with this. So, do I know the nature of who/what I am? I feel like this is a trick question. But yes…it is love.

*Good.*

Why do you ask?

*Because sometimes you forget.*

*March 27*

Good morning, God, I think I need a reminder right now. Do you ever tire of my forgetfulness? I do.

*Little one, it matters not how many times you forget. What matters is that you are willing to remember—one more time.*

Sometimes I do forget everything I know to be true about letting life unfold, about accepting what is in this moment. In this moment, I feel sad; two things come to mind. The first was a client last week whose husband died. She said, "He treated me like a princess. He was the best husband I could ask for." A part of me felt sad because I want to be treated like a princess sometimes—doted on, gushed over as if I'm so very important in my man's world. That's it. Here come the tears.

I've said to my boyfriend before that sometimes it seems like I value our relationship more than he does. And that thought leads me to if he loves me enough. He doesn't understand the spiritual principles that are the foundation of my life. God, why are we together? Could this really ever work? I am so sad right now. How did I arrive here again?

*Sandy, it's good that you are looking at it all. You've put a lot out here; let's break it down, shall we?*

Alright.

*Feeling like a princess, fitting into his life, loving you enough, why you are so sad, his not understanding you, why you are together with him, could it ever really work?*

*Simply in a nutshell, he loves you the best he is able and loves you very deeply. He shows it differently than you do. You are saddened because these thoughts that you entertained were like bad guests who won't leave. Look at them—learn from them. He understands you to the degree he understands himself.*

*Why are you together with him? Love. Acceptance. Growth.*

*Could it ever really work? Not with these thoughts you cling to. Look at all these beliefs, Sandy. They are your challenges, not his.*

Why doesn't he go through all this?

*He does—but in a different way. His challenges are more work related and children related.*

I can understand that. The main thought I want to work with is "I feel most loved when I hear romantic things said to me." And I feel empty when I don't hear them. Here we go again; I've been down this road before.

*So, let's take the trip again, shall we? Sandy, this is how you are learning like a young toddler, discovering how to walk. You are practicing holding different thoughts, and sometimes you forget. Please suspend the judgment you hold on yourself. You need a man to say romantic things to you. Is that true? What happens to you if he doesn't?*

Yes, it's true in order for the relationship to feel fulfilling. When I don't hear them, I feel empty, and then I question if this relationship is the right one for me. As I write this, something's asking me to fill my space with me. I've got lots of space, and I'm asking him to fill it. But something within me nudges me to fill it with my energy. I'm growing, and I am to expand my energy into this new space. That feels peaceful. But isn't this about any man?

*No, little one, you have seen that before. It never is about what you think it is, especially if you believe it is about someone or something outside of you.*

I do love him. Sometimes I look at him and see his innocence and that he is doing the best that he can.

*So love him, Sandy.*

But in doing this, am I just ignoring my needs?

*Little one, your needs can never be filled outside of you. That is part of human suffering—wanting and waiting for another to come and complete you.*

It's not about a man filling me? I am smiling…and laughing now.

*No, little one, it is not.*

So, let me turn this around and see if it makes sense to me. When I grow, I create additional space in my energy field that I look to fill.

*Yes.*

And I look to a man to fill it.

*Yes.*

But I should fill it with my energy, with working out, writing, cooking…

*Yes.*

I remember my completeness within. A man can add to my life—but isn't needed to complete it.

*Yes, nor do your kids need to complete it for you. Sandy, from this place, give what you think you need and don't expect anything in return. Give what you think you need. Come here first, fill yourself with what you imagine you're trying to get from another, and then give it freely.*

So, another turnaround is "I am not giving myself the kind words that I need to hear."

*Yes.*

I can see that that is true. God, how many times do I need to go through this, so I can remember again?

*Seven times. Actually, Sandy, there is no number. This is a process for you. Just understand that when you are in that space, come to me for understanding. This doesn't entail pressuring anyone to be different. Your dear friend is a beautiful soul, doing his best as you are. At any point, it is certainly alright for you to state what your wants are. Just be okay with the fact that he may not be able to give them to you.*

Like my wanting to get married again someday? I'm not even certain that is true. It just satisfies my ego—believing it will bring me a sense of security that someone will always be with me.

*And is that true?*

No, not at all. I sense I should look at something around this word *security*...about letting go of what I thought would bring me financial security. God, I think there's a lot of energy around this for me—about living in the moment and feeling secure. There are many unknowns when you are in the moment.

*Are there really? Look around you. That is all that CAN be known in this moment. It is all complete, unless your thoughts are not in this moment.*

Oh, you are good. Three beautiful birds just flew across the sky; they went out of sight, and I thought, "They no longer exist...not in this moment anyway."

*And can you see that trying to cling to the sight of them would be useless?*

Yes. I guess they were meant to be seen in the moment and enjoyed when they were there. And I shouldn't wish that they'll come back, but I should notice the next moment and what appears.

*You are good, Sandy. Witnessing...that is what you are doing. It is good practice to help you stay in the moment.*

So right now, I notice my laptop. As I look outside, I observe the shadows of some birds that just flew by. Some fly by so fast; others stop in the big pine tree and stay a while. One actually perched at the very peak like a Christmas Angel atop a tree. I feel such peace right now; I love writing so much. Thank you for the nudge back. The dream I had the other night about someone commenting on my gift of writing. It surprised me, but I do know I have a gift with words.

*Yes, you do, little one, please use it.*

Here I am asking a man to share words with me, and I'm being asked to share my words with others. Is there a connection there? I wonder if when I am not writing, I need to hear words to help me feel more secure.

*It is all connected, little one. You know how much your writing fills you. Look to fill yourself there first and notice what shifts. Let's look at this word* secure, *shall we?*

Haven't we covered that before? It feels like we did. I'm smiling because I'm thinking back to how many times I've had to cover and re-cover the same topic about feeling empty. Well, the ball is in your court. The word *secure...*

*Yes, dear one, it is a struggle for so many. Many cling to what they believe will help them to feel "secure." But what is security anyway to the human mind?*

Security—it gives people a sense of protection. People install security systems in their homes with passwords for security. We have Social Security (for now anyway). Kids drag around security blankets. So, I imagine it all involves a feeling of safety.

*From what?*

From something being taken away maybe? From feeling pain, I imagine: financial pain, relationship pain, emotional pain, or physical pain. Wow, I've never thought about it before in this way.

*And what do you know about life, Sandy?*

That we really cannot be protected from pain. But that life's stings don't have to lead to suffering. And that if I'm in pain, it signals a need to return my awareness to you for a re-alignment of thinking. I also know that nothing can be ripped away from me because of the flow of nature, the flow of life, the flow of energy. You cannot destroy energy; it simply changes form. But the mind can attach to the form, and this can cause much anxiety and stress and grief. Am I on track?

*Yes, but let's break it down and see what it may mean for you personally: financial security, emotional security, relationship security, life security.*

Financial security...would mean that I wouldn't worry about the flow of clients and that we'd be able to pay for the kids' college; it would mean that I wouldn't have to think about the flow of money; it would be available when I need it.

Emotional security…would mean that I'd never feel anything other than peace—ha ha. My feelings of insecurity, doubt, hurt, or pain would never come up. Oh, that sounds so silly.

Relationship security (promises, words, marriage) would mean that I would always be able to depend on someone being there for me. That I wouldn't ever worry about not being loved or being alone.

Life security would mean that I'd be guaranteed a long happy, healthy life, and everyone around me would be as well.

*Good, let's take a deeper look at these. You'll see where your thoughts hold you hostage. All need for security is fear-based. Security is a future thought. It can give a false guarantee. Sandy, what is promised in life?*

Birth, death, and the moments in between. It's funny, I can't really think of anything else that is guaranteed. Love isn't…until we are aware of it. Self-love isn't because not everyone chooses to feel it. Money isn't; health isn't; romance isn't; joy and peace aren't guaranteed either. It's all a choice that we make. Truly nothing is guaranteed. I'm not sure, but I want to say that God is guaranteed.

*So say it.*

God is guaranteed. But the awareness of God is not. It is a choice. Oh, that rings so true in my heart.

*So if nothing is guaranteed, then what?*

Then I can't really hold on to anything. There's nothing to protect, nothing to worry about, and nothing to fear. A sense of freedom abounds—a sense of simply being. In this space, my mind can't even attach to a concept. If nothing is promised, then I imagine anything is possible. So I imagine that it means that the future isn't guaranteed.

*Right, and where does that leave you?*

In this moment, that is all there is. This moment is the only guarantee I have because I'm in it. Then it's gone, and another one comes. A moment-by-moment guarantee—I can feel in my body where I have held onto what I thought would make me feel "secure." Now I see how I have kept myself stuck.

*Don't do anything for reasons outside of this moment. That is where expectations come from. I'll do this, so that happens. Enjoy it in the moment. Like your Zumba class, enjoy the music, the movement. Don't do it to get a better body; it may happen, it may not. Enjoy the moment. Eat in the moment. Take pleasure in others in the moment.*

I truly can feel how I've attached myself to expectations of men, of my kids, of my work…doing a specific thing, so that I'll feel a certain way. My heart is so very free. And do you know what I just decided?

*What, little one?*

That one of three things could happen regarding future finances. First, I will always make more than enough money at retirement age to comfortably support me and allow me to help my kids, or I won't physically be here at retirement age, and it won't matter how much is in my IRA anyway, or I will share my journey with someone, and together we'll be just fine financially. And you know what, God?

*What, little one?*

In this moment, I'm at peace with how my life is playing out because I know you are with me. I sense that there is more to this, but I would like to go make a cup of coffee. Can we continue this later?

*Sure, but that is not a guarantee. Just show up in the moment, and we'll see where it all goes.*

I will. Thank you for always listening to me. I love you from my whole being.

*You are my love, Sandy. Be it.*

*May 8*

Hi, God, it's been a while since I wrote. I've healed more within my heart and have experienced more moments of joy. I redecorated every room in the house since the beginning of January, and it truly feels like there's a parallel between redecorating the rooms of my house and renovating the rooms of my soul. My home is now starting to reflect how I feel inside my heart. I love the colors in every room, and I cleared out most of the clutter (ok, except in the garage!).

About a month ago, I started keeping a gratitude journal again. I found some earlier ones I'd written in as I was cleaning the basement. I reread what I'd written, and my heart felt such joy. So every day, I started writing down the moments that held joy and beauty. It lifted my spirits.

*Sandy, you understand why, don't you?*

I think it's because first, whatever I'm thinking about, I notice. So, when I look for moments that I'm grateful for, I'll see them—and lots of them. I'm capturing these moments in my heart like catching fireflies in the summertime. I'm very grateful for these moments...like the laughter that Austin and I shared in the chiropractor's office while waiting for Ariana to be treated. Or Ari's huge smile at our Zumba class when the instructor motioned for her to come up and dance next to her in front of the packed class. Moments like these are always around. I want to notice them more.

*Yes, and gratitude for these moments of joy lifts your vibration.*

So, God, I'd like to ask you about what occurred yesterday when a dear friend called to tell me that she was signing a contract with one of the largest literary agents. I felt sincerely happy for her, but I noticed that when I got off the phone, I first thought, "What am I doing wrong?" I've dreamt for a long time of having a literary agent, traveling on the Spiritual Conference circuit, appearing on TV, and being a famous author and medium.

Ugh, God, I have to ask you: Am I doing anything wrong? Is there something that is keeping all this from happening for me?

*Sandy, take a deep breath, little one.*

(Breathing…).

*Do not assume based on what you cannot see right now. You and your friend are on different timetables. Bless her and celebrate with her.*

I did, and I truly meant it. It just also triggered that part of me that thinks it should all be happening now for me as well.

*That what should be happening now?*

That my work should reach a larger audience.

*You have no idea how big your audience is. Every client that comes to you or takes one of your workshops talks to others about you.*

Thank you. I feel like this is all ego stuff rising up in me.

*It is, little one, but it is okay; let it come up. What do you think reaching a bigger audience would bring you?*

Fame. Ugh, I said it.

*And what would fame bring you?*

More people to love me. Oh, God, this is not pretty.

*And if more people loved you, then what do you imagine to be true?*

Hmmm…then I'd feel more loved and wanted.

*More loved and wanted than what?*

Than I am now…than others…it would mean I was more special.

*Sandy, here is your gift...for it is another lesson that you have been working on in this soul journey. Are you ready for truth to shine into this thought?*

I think so.

*Dearest little one, you could not be more special than you are in this moment. My love for you never changes. You do not earn a different place in my heart if you touch one person, one thousand people, or one million people. That may be hard for you to accept in this moment because your ego does not want to agree with it. But it is truth. The ego wants to keep track of numbers. My question to you is this: Are you present to the ones you are touching?*

Yes.

*And are you being true to yourself in your life with regard to your work?*

Yes, I love my work, but I do feel a continual pull to write more.

*So write more when you feel that pull as you are doing now. Notice the ease as the words flow when you allow them to, not when you think you are "supposed" to be writing. There is a flow to all of life, Sandy. You already know that. It works. The timing works. Please trust that. To answer your question, no, you are not doing anything wrong. If you were meant to be in a different place right now, life would have carried you there. It is in store for you. Let it unfold as it is supposed to. Can you trust that?*

Actually, I can. I feel that truth in my heart.

*Let it all unfold, little one. Let me repeat this again, and to all who are reading these words, let these words sink into your heart as well. If you were meant to be in a different place right now, life would have carried you there. That is true for relationships, money, work, children, and weight. Let yourselves feel the truth in these words. You are EXACTLY where you are supposed to be in this moment. Tomorrow, next week, and next year are all moments that are yet to be. When you trust that life is on your side, and you let it carry you, you can relax into the moment with peace and joy, and let it all unfold.*

Thank you. When I talked to my girlfriend Brunnie, we said the very same thing. I so love her, God, and am grateful for our friendship. She is such a beautiful light in my life.

God, why is it that sometimes I don't feel like I'm going to be here on earth for very long? When I sense that, I just want to tell everyone how much I love them and appreciate them, just in case something happens. I want people to know how I feel.

*Sandy, it is a sign of a softening heart. It is good. Continue to share your love and appreciation with all who can and will listen.*

So, to all who are reading this book, I love you. Even though we may not have met, I appreciate that you are walking this journey with me.

God, can we go back to something you said earlier? You asked me if I was being true to myself. Why did you ask that?

*Because it is of high importance in your life on your soul's agenda. Do you sense what it even means for you?*

Being true to myself—being honest with myself. Knowing what works for me and what doesn't work for me. Is that right?

*I can simplify it for you if you'd like.*

God, I love when you do that! Yes, please.

*Simply put, being true to you means doing all things with love—whether that is driving your kids to baseball and soccer, making dinner, teaching a workshop, connecting with Spirit for a client, or cleaning. Sandy, rather than focus on numbers, let this be your mantra: "All things with love."*

What just came to me was "all things with God-awareness." It's the same thing, isn't it?

*You already know the answer. So let that be your prayer: All things with love/God-awareness. We will address more about being true to yourself in other areas of your life at another time.*

Can we do it slowly? This is not always easy to go through.

*There is no rush here, Sandy…ever.*

Thank you, God, you always help me to see things from such a beautiful perspective. I love you.

*I love you too.*

*June 16*

Good morning, God, it's been a good journey since I wrote last. I've continued with the gratitude journal (except for the last few days), and it truly has affected my heart. I took my mom to Twin River casino yesterday because I didn't want her to be alone on Father's Day. We had a ball—just the two of us. I felt very present with her; there was no other place I wanted to be. Oh, there's something to that, isn't there?

*Being in the moment like there is no other place that you want to be. Yes, it is a powerful place to be: body, mind, and spirit in the same awareness, not rushing, not wishing, but simply being there.*

I notice it with my kids; when I am there fully and I bring myself wholly to the moment, I receive so much more from the moment.

*Sandy, giving and receiving are really the same when you are there fully.*

I can see that. And it feels good. I've experienced it some…more so since I've continued with my own healing. I need to ask you about what is in my heart, God.

*Go ahead; I was waiting for you to bring it up.*

It's about my work; the schedule seems lighter. Can you help me understand what is happening here? How can I best serve?

*Sandy, there is a flow to your work, right?*

Yes. I'm a little confused though. My heart feels peaceful right now, but my mind is a little concerned. Does that make sense?

*What is your mind concerned about?*

That client sessions will dry up, that my session fee is too high, that I won't have enough work to pay my bills…

*Send out an email newsletter and see what happens.*

I feel I'm missing something here—that I've not discerned why I wrote to you this morning.

*Then listen with your heart. Little one, there is nothing for you to fear there or anywhere. Let this be your prayer, "I do all things with love…all things with God." When you gain that awareness, you will remember that you have a partnering energy with you at all times: the energy of love. With love, all things are possible.*

Thank you, God. On a different note, am I missing something about my eating lately? It seems bigger than me or somehow beyond me. Like I'm not in control of my eating or I am resisting losing these last five to ten pounds.

*You are.*

Can you help me understand the resistance?

*Control.*

What do you mean control?

*Look to see how you haven't been feeling in control. As you feel that you need control, a part of you becomes anxious, is pressured, and is not comfortable. When you are uncomfortable, you tend to eat more.*
*It is also tied into your thoughts of "What if there is not enough? What if it won't be there later?" You experience this lesson in a few different areas, particularly around food, money, your kids, and your relationship. Bring yourself back to this moment; you are enough and have enough in this moment—feel it now. This moment is all you have.*

God, I release any and all anxiety to you. I give you my need to know what is going to be, and I return to peace. Thank you.

*August 6*

Wow, it's been a while, God. We've had a busy summer. Right now, I'm in Oneonta, NY, for Austin's baseball tournament, at an apartment that I've rented for the week. It is so quiet here. I brought my laptop to catch up on e-mails and I have my cell phone to return calls in the downtime. But there is no cell phone service where I'm staying and no Internet connection. So, interestingly, in this moment, I have no way to connect to anyone but you. God, I didn't mean to make you seem like a last resort…like there was no one else to turn to. I'm sorry, I don't like how that sounds.

*Sandy, my feelings aren't hurt. It is a reality for many in their lives. Actually, there may even be a bumper sticker that reads, "When there is no one to turn to, turn to God." I am a last resort for many; And that is typically when people allow me to help them "re-sort" their lives.*

I love when you do that, God! I am so happy to be here with you. I don't feel so alone here anymore…my buddy is here with me.

*I am always with you, Sandy; your "aloneness" has nothing to do with whether I am here for you or not.*

So true, so true. This just feels so different. No one can reach me here, so no one can demand anything of me, expect anything of me, or ask me to do something for them. I feel totally detached, but not in a bad way.

*And why do you think you set this trip up, for you to feel free?*

I have spent so much time pleasing others. I noticed even driving down here how much I enjoyed listening to Wayne Dyer's tapes on Intention. It was what I wanted to listen to, and I felt total peace with it. This is so odd; I feel no connection to anyone in this moment, unless I choose to bring my thoughts to someone. I feel peace. There are no disappointments, no expectations, no needs. Is this what it is like to be in Spirit? Knowing that my loved ones are fine, or I imagine that they are anyway. I trust that they are.

*What do you feel?*

Total peace.

*Then that is what it feels like to be in Spirit. Knowing, trusting—you can't be sure that Ariana didn't host a party back at home last night, but you trust that she didn't. You don't know if Austin is picking up his dorm room or is missing you or is hungry, but you trust that he has the tools to care for himself. You know your love for them, and nothing changes that.*

But if I knew they were in pain or in trouble, I wouldn't feel peace; I'd be in pain.

*Yes, but stay in this moment. They are fine. Let this be about you.*

Ok, so what do you want to talk about, God? I feel I've been summoned for a reason.

*Sandy, you summoned yourself. You needed this break for your soul. It has partly to do with your significant relationship. You were so enmeshed in it that you lost who you were again. You needed to step away—to feel who you are and to remember to not compromise that.*

Why do I lose myself like that? I know I do it, and I don't enjoy how it feels, but it is hard to separate myself when I'm in it.

*And these few days give you an opportunity to separate with love—not fear, not anger, not frustration—but with total love.*

This feels like a retreat.

*It is. Treat yourself well. Understand how you like to treat yourself—with love, kindness, and compassion. It is a time to build your heart strength.*

Heart strength?

*Yes.*

Was my heart not strong already?

*Yes. It was to a degree, but you so easily let others' wants influence your actions.*

"Fill this space with you," I hear in my head. God, I am so grateful for this time to just be. As I drove here yesterday, the thought of "I like the company of me" entered my mind. I do take pleasure in just being with myself. Help me stay true to myself, God.

*That is why you came here, Sandy. Where do you feel you are not true to yourself?*

Well, the first thing that comes to mind is with our dog, Mikey. I don't really have the time or energy that he needs, but I'm doing it for the kids, and it weighs heavily on me. With my significant relationship, I often mask my feelings, so I won't be a burden to him or so I won't feel the "rejection" when he doesn't want to talk about things. God, how do I make peace with the fact that he places no interest in my work and won't enter into any sort of discussion around it?

*Sandy, let's discuss Mikey first. Your kids want you to be happy, and they also want Mikey. Give them the responsibility of Mikey.*

But what about when they are at their dad's house?

*Let them figure it out; they are smart. Let this be their project. It will teach them responsibility for what they say they want. As for your relationship, it involves more than not having meaningful discussions about your work. You have questioned if the two of you have enough in common for this relationship to work long term.*

I don't feel that he respects my work with Spirit, and we are so different emotionally and spiritually. And my spirituality is such a big part of who I am.

*He respects you as a person, Sandy. He has no reference for your work; it is unknown to him. You have every right to share your concerns with him. Let him sit with it. Hold no fear, dear one; you will give him an opportunity to grow. He may choose to, or he may not. If he decides not to, you can then see if it moves you closer to him or not. He was bound by his past for quite some time. Your presence in his life changes him. Others can see it, even if he cannot. You help him to open his mind and his heart. Stay in love, dear one, stay in love. Let love heal your frustration.*

We often don't have similar wants or needs. We barely share any thoughts of a future together. I've brought it up in the past, usually in a frustrated or whiny way that makes me look needy.

*So what if you are?*

My fear is that if I truly ask for what I want than he would walk away.

*So let him, if he needs to do that. If the intimacy level that you ask for is too much for him, let him go, and let him let you go.*

This is not where I thought this was all going.

*Sandy, you have come to realize that you cannot change him nor does he want you to change him.*

But he is shifting, yes?

*Yes, when he wants to. Love him and understand that you need to love and honor yourself first before you are able to love him. You have a high level of passion in your relationship, with your kids, for your family, and for your work.*

God, I desire a relationship with someone who is willing to share all the parts of my life, with someone who wants a deeper connectedness of emotional and spiritual intimacy. I'm tired of trying so hard. Now I'm confused. What do I do with all this?

*Just be with it, Sandy, let it be. There is nothing to do. He is a beautiful soul and may be willing to step forward more if you give him the space to step forward in the way that he is able. It will all be okay, you'll see.*

Thank you, God. Thank you for always being here for me.

*September 21*

God, I just re-read some of our past conversations, and something struck me. Your loving words carry me to tears and provide a sense of peace in my heart repeatedly. How is it that I could expect anyone else to bring that to me?

*If they are aware of me and connect in the same way, Sandy, they could. Some are not willing to look within their hearts to forgive themselves, and they hold onto pain at a subconscious level. Some do not want to see that. You have been a teacher and student in this relationship. And I would like to address the continuous struggle if I may.*

Oh, God, please do; it is still confusing to me.

*Sandy, you live from different planes of existence. Your cores are very much the same, but the clouds of memories are different. You have an ability to tap into wisdom, to love much more easily than he knows how. He is who he is, and he feels pressure at times that he cannot live up to what you want.*

*It affects his sense of self, and he withdraws more, which impacts you and your desire for a connection. Or to put it simply, his comfort level of connectivity differs from yours. Let it all be. Come here for your connection. You may decide that as you bond with me more, you are more comfortable with his level of connectedness. Or you may decide that you want a relationship that supports you more when you are not connected. In either case, you will be okay.*

But if I choose to end this relationship, am I failing him or failing any lesson of my soul?

*Sandy, my little one, you could not fail. You have done much heart work within the confines of this relationship. Allow your heart to relax. Like a muscle that works out, it also needs rest to let it strengthen and rebuild.*

I can so relate to that; it's exactly what it feels like.

*So let it be. Don't force time together. Let the relationship find its own natural level. I think you will see how easy that can happen. Let your heart guide you. You will see, dear one, you will see.*

Thank you, God. My fear is similar to what I have felt in the past: that if I let go of this man, he would suddenly change—and the next woman he would be with would have it all with him.

*Recognize that as fear. No cruel joke is being played on you; no one stands ready to punish you for letting go. The universe is not set up that way. You know that in your heart, but a part of you doesn't buy into that.*

Thank you. That makes me feel very peaceful. God, one more thing— the flowers my client gave me in appreciation for the session I did with him. I noticed that I didn't have to do anything to receive them. He'd already paid me for the session. He sent them not because I asked or begged, but because it was in him to do that. I recognize how good it feels to receive without having to ask—it's easy. Thank you, God. I need to go take a shower. I love you.

*I love you too, Sandy. Enjoy your day.*

*October 2*

Good morning, God. I miss you even though I talk to you every day. Actually what I miss is not hearing your voice, because I haven't taken the time to listen. Honest to God, writing with you brings me to such a beautiful place.

*That is good, little one. Much is ahead for you that you cannot see, but you are starting to sense it.*

Can I know about it now?

*Not all of it.*

God, as I drove home from bringing Ariana to school, I thought of the evolution of this dialog with you; it's shifted. Like feeding a baby, a baby's digestive system can only tolerate its mom's milk or formula at first…then gradually, it can digest more.

*Yes, and that is why you are able to receive different ideas and pieces of wisdom at each stage of your soul's journey. You can absorb more now than you could've when we first started.*

So, what would you like to share with me now?

*Only love.*

For some reason, I knew that would be your answer. God, I'm noticing the concepts of love being at our core, love as the greatest healer. There is only one of us here; this seems to resonate all around me—in emails I receive or songs I hear, etc.

*It is truth.*

Women have begun sharing with me how happy they are in their new relationships…so, so very happy, and they want every woman to experience what they feel. I wonder if that is a message for me.

*Sandy, if it resonates with you, it is a message for you. We are all over the board this morning, aren't we? The beauty of your mind…*

I know. I get excited about so many ideas when I write with you. So, where would you like to start?

*Sandy, you asked about some issues that are surfacing for you. You've discerned in your heart the tug to speak to larger groups, to be the messenger you know you were destined to be. Continue to release any thoughts of fear or worry or any other blocks and allow it to unfold. It is on its way. Follow the inspiration that comes to you. It will lead you, guide you, and help you to unfold your journey perfectly.*

Thank you. So, hold no thoughts of worry about a lighter schedule?

*That's right; it will provide you with an opportunity to gather materials together like a speaker's packet; you've thought about this but have put it off. This would be a good time to bring it to the forefront.*

Ok, thank you! I know that I have much to share. And I know Spirit has a lot to share. I've always wanted to be a spokesperson for a company. So maybe I'll be a "Spokesperson for Spirit"; I like that. What do you think about that idea?

*See how it feels to you.*

I am very excited about it! It feels uplifting.

*Then let it become real for you. There is much support here for you to step into that role.*

I know that Spirit wants to help us here. God, when I tell people that, do you feel—and I even feel silly asking this—but do you feel insulted?

*Sandy, my dearest little angel, do you see Spirit as separate from me?*

No, I see you as the ultimate of love.

*So if people can resonate with the idea of Spirit helping them return to love, wonderful. If people resonate more with the idea of me helping them return to love, wonderful. I am not jealous, if that is what you were asking. I don't do jealous. Love is love, and however one wants to return to it (or remember that it is what they were created as) makes no difference to me. You are not saying that this way is the only way. There are many—many paths to love, many paths to me.*

But what about Jesus being the only way to you? I've struggled with that in the past. Some religious teachers adamantly preach that Jesus is the only way.

*Jesus is the only way for their teaching. He realized more of me within him. You all have the capability to do so as well. Old time teachings needed the separation. It helped to bring order to chaos—to keep people in line.*

Thank you, God. Can we continue this later? I haven't been to the gym in a week and feel like I need to do that. But I'll be back later. I love you, God.

*I love you, little one. Drive in peace.*

*October 9*

Hi, God, it has been almost a month now since I stumbled across a Hawaiian healing technique 'ho'oponopono,' which involves shifting our perspective when we see a challenge or problem in another person or in the world. It suggests that something within us responds and facilitates the healing. So, I've worked with the technique and found that it really entails transmuting any worry, stress, or irritation…and healing it back to peace and love.

The four statements to the technique—"I love you; I'm sorry; please forgive me; and thank you"— profoundly affect me. I say them all the time. And I know I speak them to you—that I love you. I apologize for viewing any part of my life in any way other than from love, which is my essence. Please forgive me for forgetting in the moment. Thank you. It transforms something inside. It releases me from the energy that is toxic, and I quickly return to peace.

God, you probably already know this, but I wanted to share a part of an email that I sent to Brunnie the other day:

"Brunnie, I'm doing some good writing, and I think I know who my soul mate really is…ready? It's God. He's always there for me with an understanding word, gentleness, comfort, guidance, wisdom, and humor. Now if he just had a body!"

God, you are. You are my soul mate. All my life I've wondered if I'd ever find him and felt frustration that I wasn't manifesting him, and there you were all the time. I love you. And I'm sorry that I didn't know it or realize it until now. You have always been there for me. I don't even know if I have the words for it. But I want others to know it and to feel it.

*That sounds just like what those women said to you. You already have it—with me.*

It even affects my significant relationship. I realized last Saturday that I don't need him to be anything different for me; our relationship is what it is, and I finally understand that he does the best that he can, putting what he is able to into our relationship. It's not a close relationship during the week, but I have other friends I can share special moments with during the week.

I have such peace right now. And I know that no matter if he and I stay together or if we go our separate ways, I will be able to do so with peace, love, and gratitude. I am in the moment with it all right now, and I am okay with whatever is meant to be because I trust that you are with me and that you are for me. Thank you for how you've helped me, how you've gently loved me back to peace, to love.

*Sandy, it was within you all the time; you just didn't know it. I was able to guide you because you were willing to be guided—baby steps, with as much as you were able to do in the moment.*

Oh, God, as I look back, I spent a lot of time complaining, whining, and enduring the stress of what I thought I wanted but didn't have. I have it all. I really do. And you are my source.

*I am that I am. You have done well recently at forgiving yourself for not knowing during this growth period. It was not an easy journey for you, little one, but you stayed the course, coming to this space for guidance, inspiration, and doing your best in practicing to heal what didn't resonate with love.*

God, how can I help people experience this? I want to help whomever I am able to make this journey back to love. Please show me the way.

*Let people read your writings, Sandy. They will see themselves in your humanness.*

*October 17*

God, I miss you already! A few days ago, I believed I had completed this book. I felt like crying because I didn't want this closeness to be over.

*Why would it end, little one?*

I know it sounds silly now, but I guess I believed that maybe you would only be available to me to write this book?

*Sandy, do you really think that to be true? This dialog is never ending, if you'd like.*

Ok…so please don't ever leave me.

*How could I, little one?*

I know, I know, you can't because I am you, you are me, and we are one. This is a continual journey of remembering, isn't it?

*Yes, it is. Not all are willing to take the time, and as a result, they see what is not "right" with their lives and feel pain.*

God, I fell into that a little bit yesterday. I've realized how crucial it is for me to connect with you in order to feel a sense of "all is well." Just knowing you're here right now, I feel peace. And I love who I am when my heart is open.

*So what causes you to close your heart, Sandy?*

Ugh, I thought I was done with all this, no?

*Done with all what?*

Done looking inside myself. Sorry. Seriously, God, I'm open to anything that I am meant to look at, so that I can be more of you here.

*First, you cannot be more of me here because you already are me here—you just didn't know it. This involves allowing your awareness to help you remember who you already are in mind, body, and spirit.*

Wait, in body? You don't have a body.

*I do through you…and through each and every human walking the earth. Most people just don't know it. So I actually have many bodies. But before we go into that, what causes you to close your heart, Sandy?*

When I offer love that is not received or reciprocated, when I look for (oh, here it is) validation or appreciation and it is not there, I feel my heart wanting to close.

*And then what happens?*

I am quiet and feel rejection, and then I don't feel like giving of myself there anymore. God, I know you're going to ask, "Why do you look to others for that?"

*It was going to be something similar to that.*

It is such a human part of me—to want to feel that back from others. Doesn't everyone want that?

*Most do. Some move beyond that…when they gain awareness that when others do not reciprocate, it is not about them at all. Sandy, the sun shines because…*

Because that is what it does.

*Yes. And do you imagine that the sun cares at all if someone stays indoors so as not to feel it or shades themselves from the sun? Does the sun stop shining in response? Or does it continue to shine?*

It continues to shine because that is how it was created and what it was created for. God, I see where you're going. You are good.

*And I see where you're going too, and you're good too, little one. The sun is what it is, and it does what it does without effort. And so can you all, in any moment that you choose to wake up. You all took this journey to return to your loving essence. But you've forgotten in many moments because pain, guilt, worry, fear, or doubt have become such distractions…until they are not anymore.*

*It is not in your highest and best to judge yourself each time you are distracted by the humanness in you. Delight in it: "Oh, here I am again!" You can meet that part of yourself with gentle eyes and a loving heart, and then you'll return to love. Forgive yourself for the journey you've taken. All roads lead back home.*

I can see that, God. I can also see how quickly I return home to you. Thank you for the reminder that no matter which path one takes, there is an opportunity for all to come back home to love.

*You will help them, Sandy.*

I will do my best, God.

*Take out the comma.*

Huh? Oh. "I will do my best God." Is that what you mean?

*Yes.*

It sounds like I'll do my best God impersonation.

*You are funny.*

Holy moly, you're amazing. You just had me look at that last sentence as "I'll do my best 'God in person' nation." Bringing God into my person for the nation?

*I knew you would get it.*

I am so in awe of you. I don't know what to say right now.

*So, let me have the floor, so to speak. Let it sink in, Sandy. It will take a while for you and others to fully absorb what I am about to say.*

*The time has come for all to remember. You destroy yourselves and one another. The time has come to remember, so that you can create the heaven on earth that you all agreed to. Stop fighting inside yourselves, and you'll cease the fighting that you see outside of you. The inner wars that rage against your own self are what you see projected outside of you. Put down your weapons of **self-destruction** and you will see the world follow suit. The world reflects your inner world. You want to see change out there first. Change within you first.*

*Forgive. Love. Allow me to shine the light into every hurt, every worry, and every fear. Bring it forward. There is nothing too dark that the light of forgiveness and love couldn't heal. Some of you don't believe me. But I never left you.*

*Come home to forgiveness. Come home to peace. Come home to love. It doesn't mean that you have to physically die in order to come home. You can do it right there in your bodies. Hear me now. **I love you. I am sorry that you thought I left you, that you may have thought I didn't care, that you may have felt that I didn't show up for you in the way you wanted. Please forgive me. Thank you.***

God, you've done nothing wrong. Why would you need to apologize?

*Sandy, it's what many need to hear and feel in order to move forward.*

I am still speechless. This is so unheard of—that God would apologize to us. It is so contrary to what religions have taught that we are so low in comparison to you, that we are to bow in front of you. So much is unraveling inside me right now. I can feel it just by reading what you wrote. I am humbled, God, by reading it—that you would say I'm sorry. You're meeting people right where they are. That's it, isn't it?

*Yes.*

You are the best, God. I don't know what to write. I need to be with this to allow it to sink in. You want to meet people where they are. That is what you did for me in the last two years with this dialog. And when you meet people in that way, there is nothing left to fight against, is there?

*No.*

I love you.

*I love you too. Be my voice, Sandy. Meet them where they are. Help them hear my voice.*

*October 19*

Good morning, God. In August, when I was in Cooperstown, and we dialogued together, you asked me which areas in my life were perhaps out of alignment. One of my answers was our dog, Mikey. I have known that Mikey needs more attention than we give him. With my work schedule, the kids' schedule, and the time I spend away from here, Mikey is alone too much. It's not fair to him. So back then, you suggested that I have the kids take more responsibility for him, which they did for a little while, and then things returned to the way they were previously.

*This often happens when change is not initiated from within.*

So after that, the kids and I agreed that it would be best to find a new home for Mikey. I've wondered where would be best for him. And a couple days ago, my friend Heather said her sister-in-law was searching for a new small dog to keep her other dog company.

Today I am delivering Mikey to his new owners. It has been an emotional experience. Ari and Austin kept asking me to change my mind, and through my tears, I held to my decision. Packing up his stuff last night, I sobbed as I looked at the package of dog biscuits that had a likeness of his face on the front of the box!

God, I'm conflicted right now. On the one hand, I am very grateful to Heather's sister-in-law and that the opportunity came to me—I didn't have to go search it out. But on the other hand, this is so difficult. Is what I'm doing best for Mikey? Am I doing what is best for my kids? Or am I just doing what is best for me? I feel like I'm failing my kids because I am

174

not willing to keep Mikey. I feel a little silly that this is something I'm bringing to you. But help me to see this more clearly please.

*Sandy, you know in your heart that if you changed your mind to stop the tears of your kids, you would be prolonging the inevitable, right?*

Yes, I do imagine that.

*And you do know that this is not just about Mikey but about allowing change to move through your life. Releasing what you thought was supposed to be. It's not always easy, little one. It entails letting go of control.*

What do you mean, letting go of control? Of Mikey? I'm confused.

*Control of what your kids feel. You allow them to feel sadness and are there for them, letting them move through it in the way they are able. And you support them, loving them through it. Remember how Austin showed you that the other day?*

Yes, after school the other day, when I told him that Heather knew of a perfect home for Mikey, Austin barraged me with all these what-if's: "Mommy, what if they don't take him for walks?" (Ok, that didn't make sense because we hardly ever took him for walks; he would just run around in our huge backyard.) "Mom, what if they decide they don't like him? What if they don't get the right kind of food for him?" What if, what if, what if—after the fifth or sixth what-if, I said, probably with a little irritation in my voice, "Austin, you're not making sense right now, honey."

*And remember how he responded.*

He said, "Mommy, so let me not make sense right now." Touché. I hugged him tight and apologized right away. I told him he didn't have to make sense for me. He was doing his best to make sense of a situation that he doesn't even want to deal with.

*Life doesn't always make sense. You know that.*

I do. I told Austin that I moved through Talia's death, and we survived a divorce and Papa's death. I knew we would somehow get through this. I'm not sure it made him feel any better, but I know it helped me by remembering that. So, back to my question—am I doing the right thing? Am I being selfish by not keeping him? My sisters and my friends have all told me I'm doing the right thing, but a part of me feels like I'm failing my kids by not keeping Mikey for them. And I needed to hear from you. It's like you hold the truth for me.

*Take a deep breath, Sandy.*

(Breathing)

*Are you doing the right thing? It's only partially about Mikey. There are many opportunities for learning and healing here. Mikey was the form that you are learning and healing through. Let's break it down, shall we?*

Please do.

*First, your question of "Am I doing the right thing?" Sandy, look at how you define what is "right" and "wrong."*

Is it what I am supposed to do?

*There is no "supposed to do." There are your actions, and there are lessons and gifts with every result from your action. In this case, you want to do what is best for your dog. Your action is out of love for him. He'll be fine.*

If I'm truly honest, yes, it is out of love for him, but also a little bit out of frustration that I had to keep cleaning up after him because he still had many accidents.

*And he had accidents because no one was there for him.*

Yes.

*So, you are moving him to a place where people will be there for him more, right?*

Yes.

*And that would be good for him, yes?*

Yes…I am able to embrace it now.

*As far as your being selfish for not keeping him. This circumstance triggers some leftover energy from your divorce, little one—that you couldn't/wouldn't stay together for the kids.*

Ugh. I can feel that.

*Are they well balanced?*

Yes.

*Do they have joy?*

Yes, in most moments (except lately, because of this situation with Mikey).

*Your fear, little one, is an old one that says you are solely responsible for your children's happiness. You have seen that despite your attempts to make them happy, they can still choose to not be happy, right?*

Yes.

*And have you also seen their resiliency; through divorce, through moving, through the loss of their grandfather, that they are able to feel tremendous joy, peace, love, and compassion?*

Yes.

*You are helping them to realize that life may not always go as planned, and you are helping them to know and utilize the tools of fully being present with what they are feeling—to move through it all. You are a good model for them.*

Thank you, God.

*And this idea that you have somehow "failed" them. Many people have believed that I "failed" them when they do not receive what they prayed for, what they so desperately wanted. They only see part of the picture as your kids do now. They only witness their feelings of sadness, but they are even able to break through their sadness with the understanding that this is best for Mikey.*

Yes, they are. They are both so loving and compassionate. I love them with all of my heart. They are both remarkable kids; I am so proud of them. Thank you, God, for helping me through this.

*Any time, little one. All is well. You are not seeing yet how this will free more of your energy to be present to your children.*

Ok, I do not understand that in this moment, but thank you, I think! My heart feels peaceful again. Thank you, God.

*October 20*

Hi, God, things feel so different without Mikey here. Austin cried a little bit before school because Mikey usually runs to greet him when he wakes up, and Austin missed that. But when he returned home from school, we enjoyed a nice talk, and he seems to be doing pretty well. I noticed this morning as I cleaned the house a little bit that I am able to open the doors to all the rooms now. I had to keep both kids' doors closed and the bathroom door closed because Mikey would run in there and either root around in the trash or pee on the floor. The idea of "doors now opening"…feels significant to me.

*It is, little one. Not necessarily because of Mikey, but it is in your whole life right now. Many opportunities are being presented to you because your energy is ready for them. Notice the ease at which things come into alignment.*

I do notice that. And I am amazed at what is now happening with little effort. A couple weeks ago, my dear friend and soul sister Maureen Hancock ("The Comedian Medium") referred me to a producer looking for a Spirit medium to be part of a potential TV series! We just filmed the pilot for it, and it went really well. I gave the producer a copy of *Congratulations…It's an Angel*, and after she read it, she phoned and said, "Sandy, this has to be a best seller!" She referred me to a literary agent (which I'd been praying for) who wants to see all that I've written. God, these are things I've longed for…why now?

*You are moving into a phase of your life where you live more from the vibration of love. Like those in Spirit, the lag time of creation is much less.*

*In other words, your thoughts will manifest more easily with less effort, in less time. It is available to all who are willing to clear the lower vibrations of toxic thought from their energy field.*

I can sense that. Thanks, God, I'd love to stay and write more with you, but I have to return to the office. I'll be back in a few hours.

*I'll be here.*

*October 22*

It's been three days since Mikey left, and things here in this house are peaceful; the kids and I laugh together more. I am no longer irritated at Mikey for being so needy (I almost hesitate to write that because I wonder if you'll tell me that he mirrored my neediness). But I no longer feel guilty anytime I leave the house. I really do feel free, and the kids seem fine with it all. Thank you, God, for helping me to see that it really was the best thing not only for Mikey, but for us as well. I'm a happier mom, and I'm more present with my kids.

*Do you want me to not address the "neediness" part? It is significant, little one. But we don't have to go there if you don't want to. I never force.*

Of course, we can go there. I know you always do it out of love.

*Your writing in the last few months has held an energy of neediness, correct? Of wanting more attention in your relationship? Little one, Mikey mirrored you.*

But now he's not here…so what does that mean?

*That you healed that part of you and you no longer need to see it reflected in your immediate world.*

So that is why I gave Mikey to his new home?

*It is a part of it on a subconscious level. You all attract what is within you. So it would make sense that your dog, Sandy, would be similar to what you didn't want to see in yourself.*

So even animals play a role in helping us to heal parts of ourselves?

*Only always.*

Wow. Do you know what else I realized? That the **fear** of the sadness that I imagined we'd have to feel was much worse than the sadness we all felt.

*Did you just see what you wrote? Write it again.*

The **fear** of the sadness that I imagined we'd feel was much worse than the actual sadness we all felt.

*Beautifully said, Sandy. And that fear keeps people stuck in jobs, relationships, addictions, and unhealthy behaviors—the fear of what they imagine they would have to feel.*

Thanks, God, I'm going to go to bed now. Thank you for being you.

*I am you, you are me, and we are one. Now go to bed, little one.*

One more thing, God. Are we done with this book?

*Does it feel complete to you?*

The struggle feels like it's over, God. I want to cry, and I'm not sure why. It seems like I made it through the war, and I'm coming home.

*You did, little one. Welcome home...to your heart. And please remember one thing: This dialog doesn't ever need to end.*

I love you, God.

*I am here for always, in all ways, for always. Let's enjoy the journey together—it is a journey that has no end.*

# EPILOGUE

To the reader...reflections from Sandy...
I'm grateful to you, for taking this journey with me. It has been about a year since this manuscript was complete, and it is going to press as I write this. I feel like I've been pregnant with the dream of getting these messages out, and I am finally going to give birth to it! I felt each and every painful "contraction" as I let God love me through every layer of fear and confusion I'd held. I still forget from time to time, and then remember to let God lovingly bring me back into a place where fear doesn't exist.

I'm laughing to myself, because I'm hearing God's thoughts as I'm typing this. And I'm silently saying, "Heyyy, these final thoughts are supposed to be mine!" (What was I thinking?? LOL) I'm hearing, *"See the 'contractions' as simply "contradictions to who you really are"*. Okay, I'm still learning that when God places something in my heart, I make room for it and let it grow.

I'm honored to be a vehicle for Divine Love in whatever way I am called. We're working on *"What was God Thinking?!"* Book 2, as well as a couple of other book projects. I've been invited to share my journey with many audiences, the healing practice is expanding, and I've witnessed more powerful shifts within my clients when they are ready to ask God the most hidden questions of their hearts... "Am I worthy, God? Did I fail? Am I enough?" I am in awe of the power of God's love to heal.

The relationship that I wrote so much about came to an end. I've never liked goodbyes, and this one was no different. It took over a year for us to let go, and allow the relationship to transition into what it is now...a close, loving friendship. He recently shared with me that being with me "softened" him and that he was grateful for that. I imagine that was partly why I was in his life. Maybe relationships don't really ever end... maybe they just change form, and find the place they are meant to be in our hearts.

When that relationship shifted, I was feeling a little antsy, processing sadness, questioning what I really wanted in life, and I had way too much time on my hands, especially when my kids were with their dad. I decided I needed a hobby. So, I persuaded my daughter to go to the crafts store with me, because I thought I'd try painting. As I walked through the acrylic paint aisle, my cart quickly became the new home to paints, brushes, an easel, and a few canvasses. Quite honestly, I didn't know what I was doing. My daughter, said, "Mom, are you SURE you're really going to do this? You're spending a lot of money on this stuff...and you've never done this before!" I know I can be impulsive from time to time, but there was a nudging in my heart that I just HAD to follow. In 5 months, I painted over 40 paintings, had an art show, and actually started writing poetry! I felt so fulfilled and happy with this new-found creative energy flowing through me. Maybe an "ending" isn't really an ending...maybe it is just an opening of a door that you couldn't see before.

So, my friends, what about you? What tender places in your heart did this book take you to? Did it inspire you to have your own loving dialog with God? I'd love to hear your stories. If you haven't done it yet, maybe it's time to make some time for it. You are worthy. Go, try it. Finish this book, (you're almost there) take some deep breaths, and tune into your heart... then share this moment, and whatever is in it, with God...and allow the response. What would God want you to know? Maybe it's time to ask.

*I've been waiting for you.*

Stand in your moment...
by Sandy Alemian

Life's challenges knock at your door.

You cover your ears, so you don't have to hear the persistent knocking, of cancer, of death, of addiction.

You cover your eyes, so you don't have to see the pain, the struggle of those you love.

You cover your heart, so you don't have to feel the agony of life slipping away.

And yet, no matter how hard you try to fight for them...babies die, cancer breathes one's last breath, addiction colors life in shades of grays and blacks.

No matter how hard you fight to not feel, your walls crash down...and you are seen shaking, stripped down, exposed, naked, vulnerable.

The choice is to run for cover...or stand in your moment.

If you run, you run for what seems an eternity, darting from pain, so it won't ever, ever touch the wound that was never allowed to heal.

If you stand in your moment, you may begin to hear that still, small voice whisper, "I love you. I've never left you."

If you stand in your moment, you may begin to see others who are also standing in their own vulnerability, and you no longer feel alone...you begin to move toward each other, drawn to one another by interconnected heartstrings of compassion...and hope.

If you stand in your moment, you may begin to feel the beat of your own heart...that is beating in unison with the heart of God...and the heart of all of mankind.

You may begin to remember that when nothing is certain, anything is possible, that healing can happen, and that it's possible that one's life never ends, but simply changes form.

You may begin to know that perhaps the journey has called you to stand in each moment, to dance with the unknown, to learn and grow with grace, and then reach out with compassion.

You may begin to feel grateful that even one person's life has breathed easier, just because you have lived.

And then we may begin to dance together...knowing that we can help each other come home again to love...again, and again, and again.

May you stand in your moment.

## About the Author:

Sandy Alemian is an Inspirational Speaker, Certified Bereavement Facilitator and well-respected Spirit Medium. "What was God thinking?!" is her second book. Sandy is a vehicle of hope, love, truth and healing in the world, through her written and spoken word. She inspires and empowers her audiences to move through some of life's most challenging experiences. Sandy provides insights and guidance through messages she receives from God, Angels and our loved ones in Spirit. Her passion is to help others to heal old beliefs and emotions, freeing themselves from repeating stressful, painful and fearful patterns. As a result, clients and readers alike experience life more fully, find reasons to believe in themselves, and bring a greater sense of harmony into their lives. Sandy lives in Massachusetts with her two children. Her website is: www.sandyalemian.com